6/16

100 q

- Embroidery

Designing for Embroidery
from Ancient and Primitive Sources

Designing for Embroidery
from Ancient and Primitive Sources

by Jan Messent

Studio Vista
London

Acknowledgements

Willing and enthusiastic friends were never more appreciated than those who helped me with the preparation of this book. My particular thanks go out to two dear friends, Gene and Cynthia Sparks—Gene for taking the photographs so beautifully, and Cynthia for her indispensable help and advice. Their kindness flowed freely and gladly even while preparing to move to the other side of the world. My sincere thanks are also due to Alan Marsh, who assisted Gene with the photography, to Roma Scrivener who typed the manuscript with skill and patience, and to Val Harding whose help and enthusiasm have been invaluable.

I am deeply indebted to my embroidery friends, who generously allowed me to use examples of their work to illustrate my ideas, and to Peter Narracott, of the Pitt-Rivers Museum, Oxford, who was of great help to me in my research and quest for photographs.

My thanks finally to my husband and children, whose interest and love have made the experience so pleasurable.

Studio Vista
an imprint of Cassell & Collier Macmillan Publishers Ltd,
35 Red Lion Square, London WC1R 4SG,
and at Sydney, Auckland, Toronto, Johannesburg,
an affiliate of Macmillan Inc., New York

Copyright © Jan Messent 1976
First published in the UK by Studio Vista, a division of
Cassell and Collier Macmillan Publishers Limited
First printing 1976

ISBN 0 289 70600 9

Set in Plantin 113
Printed by Colour Reproductions Ltd., Billericay, Essex.
Bound by R. J. Acfords Ltd., Chichester, Sussex.

Contents

Acknowledgements
Introduction

Part I
Materials, techniques and designing
The purpose   9
Materials   10
The use of found objects   12
Techniques   14
About primitive designs   29
Where to look   30
How to look   32
Some ways of making a design   34
Methods of designing   44
The case of the 'already perfect' design   46

Part II
Source material and inspiration
Ancient civilizations   47
Ethnic sources   66
Signs, symbols and objects   78
Bibliography   126
Suppliers   127
Index   128

Introduction

My aim is to introduce embroiderers to the wonderful sources of design available to them from the world of primitive and ancient art, and at the same time to offer some practical assistance in overcoming the stumbling-block of many a competent embroiderer—making designs from source material. It is not my intention to offer ready-made designs, and my ideas merely suggest possible ways of interpreting the design material. Everyone who designs (and that inevitably includes all embroiderers) will produce something quite different from the next person, even though they may be using the same source of inspiration. In many cases I have suggested suitable techniques to use, but these only represent just a few of the many possibilities open to the embroiderer. I leave it to you to make your own choice of techniques.

I have purposely avoided using actual embroidery designs as inspiration, although I have included other textiles such as weaving and rug-making. To try to reproduce the exact style and method of embroidery of hundreds of years ago will not advance the craft today. We must look for design ideas which can be used in the modern idiom, and find a new way of expressing ourselves in embroidery whether the source of the design is recognizable or not. This does not mean, of course, that we cannot use traditional stitches and methods. On the contrary, most of the stitches we use today are very ancient indeed, and some of the methods of using yarns, fibres and fabrics date back to thousands of years before Christ. Rug-making and weaving methods have changed very little, although machines have been introduced in 'civilized' countries to speed up the production process. Embroiderers still use some of the stitches seen on the superb embroideries of ancient Peru, though many of their weaving techniques were too complex for modern

weavers to emulate. The embroiderer can, however, use ancient and primitive techniques in ways which reflect the times in which we live—by producing the kind of design we can live with comfortably, selecting the colours we enjoy seeing most (which were often not obtainable in ancient times), and by using fibres which were not known then but which we find so interesting and convenient to use nowadays.

There are many ways of preparing to make a design for embroidery—so many, in fact, that no one need say, as many do, that although they can embroider they cannot design. Although the same design, with certain alterations, can be used in many different ways, it is necessary to understand the various methods of designing in order to give greater scope to the skill of the embroiderer in a wider variety of treatments.

Many embroiderers have not yet started to explore the design sources of ancient and primitive people, since the trend in recent years has been one of abstract design and designs from nature. Some people might call it cheating to use what has already been used on a textile or on an ancient piece of jewelry, but they are probably misinterpreting the idea as blind copying. What the embroiderer *may* do quite ethically is to use these designs as sources of inspiration, as a starting point from which to develop creative ideas, specifically for embroidery.

In this book I use the term 'embroidery' loosely, and in the modern sense of the word, to mean a creative art using *any* yarn and fabric technique, including not only the many forms of traditional stitchery but also macramé, off-loom weaving, knitting, crochet, rug-hooking, tufting and soft toy-making. The styles of ancient and primitive art are so varied that all these methods can be employed to interpret them, and perhaps others

1
Hanging Things by the author. Inspired by the colourful atmosphere of a Tunisian or Moroccan bazaar, festooned with clothing and carpets, this piece required very little equipment and, for anyone who knows the basic knitting and crochet stitches, is easy to make.

7

too which you can invent for yourself. African and Pacific masks, for instance, are wonderful sources of inspiration for those interested in macramé as well as stitchery, and they provide a good opportunity to work in both these methods on the same piece of work. Long, hanging pieces of twine or nylon thread with gaily coloured beads and feathers, with a face embroidered on canvas or knitted, would express perfectly the essential characteristics of one of these masks.

Because of the vast range of subject matter available, there are many areas of ancient and primitive art which I have not been able to include, and others which I have mentioned only briefly. However, this book is intended to be a starting-point and an inspirational guide, not an exhaustive reference work, and it is my hope that you will use the Bibliography to seek further information, for what better way of planning an embroidery than by doing a little historical research at the same time? If the ideas in this book introduce you to the fascination of ancient history and of ethnology, then the preparation of it will have been well worthwhile.

Part I
Materials, techniques and designing

1 The purpose

I find that I am often asked by non-embroiderers, 'What is it for?' or, worse still, 'What do you call it?' The only sensible reply you can give is that you are a creative person and that what you are doing is in the nature of a creative and pleasurable exercise using fabrics and threads, in the same way that a chef or a painter exercises his own creative talents. Do not think that you must always have a good practical reason for making a piece of embroidery; a natural desire to create something tangible, exciting and beautiful is sufficient. You may well see in it, after completion, mistakes in design and construction which you will not make again; put these mistakes down to experience. Like any art form, trial and error is involved to a large extent.

A drawing of one of the Isle of Lewis Chessmen. These chessmen are used as the basis of a design in Chapter 11 (See page 63).

2 Materials

Nowadays a very wide variety of materials, natural and synthetic, is used in the textile crafts and particularly in embroidery. The variety of techniques available to the embroiderer allows more scope in the use of 'difficult' materials than is possible for, say, the weaver. However, do resist the temptation to use too many good ideas on one piece of work; this maxim applies throughout the whole field of embroidery.

Fibre, thread and yarn

These terms are sometimes used rather indiscriminately, and it is useful to know exactly what they mean. Fibre is the basic material (for instance, the fleece of a sheep, or the hairy part of a coconut shell) which is then spun into thread or yarn. A number of individual threads may be plied together to form a thicker yarn (3-ply wool, for instance, consists of three threads plied together).

The longer the embroiderer has practised her craft, the more materials she will have available — sometimes enough to complete a piece of work. However, always be on the lookout for new materials: odd balls of wool and remnants to be picked up cheaply, pieces begged from friends, or exchanged, and leftovers from sewing and knitting. Mail order firms which specialise in yarns of all types always have sample cards and price lists available. It is worthwhile collecting these and keeping them for reference, as the qualities and colours stocked by these firms are not available in shops. Look for their addresses in needlework and craft magazines, and in the list of suppliers at the back of the book. New embroiderers should experiment with as many different materials as they can. Here are some, both usual and unusual; and there are very many others.

Wools

Wool is available in a great range of qualities and thicknesses, for instance crewel and knitting wools in all plys, wool and synthetic mixtures, and mixtures containing lurex threads; fancy textured yarns containing lumps and bumps, flecks, and two or three colours twisted together; handspun wool, dyed or undyed; and very thick rug wool. Rug thrums can be bought by the pound from carpet factories — these are useful lengths, available cheaply in all shades.

Handspun wool and hair

Sheep's wool and hair from all kinds of animals can be spun successfully on a hand spindle with a little practice. Hair and fur are easier to handle if first mixed with a little sheep's fleece at the carding stage. Do not wash it before spinning; it is easier to spin it while still containing its own natural grease.

Silks, cottons and crochet threads

These are manufactured in beautiful colours, and range in thickness from fine to quite heavy, stranded and twisted. Button thread is just as useful as expensive silk. Crochet thread can be obtained in a wide variety of colours and thicknesses.

Metal threads

Specialist embroidery shops supply real gold and silver threads, which are expensive, but their effect is remarkably beautiful when used with skill and good taste. They are usually couched on to fabric. Lurex threads are cheaper, and can be used together with other yarns to provide a sparkle in embroidery, knitting or crochet. Heavier types have been twisted with cotton, and can be used alone.

Cords

Cords are made from plastic, nylon and other synthetics. Cotton piping cord, available in various thicknesses, is useful because it dyes well.

Twine and string

These can be cotton, jute, or the coloured synthetic kind used for parcels. Leather thonging and raffia can also be used.

Nylon tights and stockings

Cut into strips, these are very useful for any of the rug-hooking techniques. They can be bleached by boiling, and they take nylon dye easily.

Nylon and synthetic yarns

These play a useful part in embroidery, for they have a unique quality which imparts lustre and sparkle to a piece of work.

Unspun fibres

Jute, flax, animal wool and hair, and synthetics having a reasonable long staple can be used where a shaggy pile or an unusual textural effect is required, for instance in rug-hooking, couching and tufting.

3 The use of found objects

Every embroiderer who likes to experiment collects what are known as 'found objects', to see if something other than the conventional needle and thread can be used constructively in a design.

In the photograph are various metal objects: a watch-spring and wheels, metal gauze, washers, studs and turnings from a lathe are all effective materials for use in metal thread embroidery. Wooden objects illustrated include the large curtain ring at the top; flat lollipop sticks, which are very useful on small weaving projects; beads of various sizes; and flat discs, which are very good for covering with needleweaving. Plastic objects are very useful, particularly curtain rings, flat rings from the centres of rolls of adhesive tapes, plastic-net vegetable and fruit bags, sequin waste, washers and small plastic lollipop sticks. Melon seeds, shells, polished gemstones, acorn cups, artificial flower stamens and little foam-rubber shapes are just a selection of the many other items which can be used to give an added dimension to a piece of embroidery by covering, clustering, hanging, or stitching over.

Often, the acquisition of these bits and pieces plays an important part in determining the concept of a piece of work and the method to be used on it. This can be an exciting way to begin, knowing that what you intend to use is intrinsic to the whole idea and will not be stuck on as an afterthought or as a last desperate measure to make the piece more interesting. So try to plan the use of your found objects right at the beginning, when you plan your colours and materials; you can then see whether found objects are likely to help the design, and if you have too many or too few. This last point is a danger which most embroiderers have to wrestle with — the danger of using too many objects on one piece in the hope that all our ideas will work, or of not using enough and thereby making an insignificant, perhaps odd-looking statement. Generally speaking, objects of one particular kind look effective together as long as there are enough of them, and they are used with care and sensitivity; in other words, various types of rings, hoops and other round objects can be used together, or bits and pieces made of the same material, such as wood-shavings, wooden beads and discs.

Whatever you do, do not use found objects to express their natural function — sea-shells to indicate a sea-shore, for instance, snail-shells for the back of a snail, feathers for a bird, or real seeds for a cross-section of a fruit. This is quite pointless, as it should be within the scope of the embroiderer to find a new way of expressing all these forms *in design* without resorting to a representational approach.

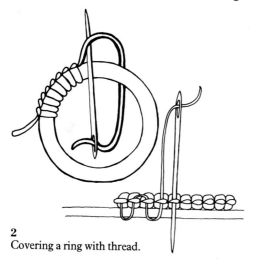

2
Covering a ring with thread.

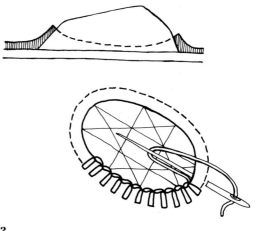

3
Holding down a stone or jewel.

12

4
Collection of found objects.

5
Covering a ring with leather or fabric.

6
Various ways of attaching sequins.

13

4 Techniques

In primitive societies, both past and present, the techniques used to express ideas dictate the style of ornament to a large extent; the same is true of embroidery, and the method of expressing a design must be chosen with care, sometimes by adapting a technique and sometimes by altering the design. For this reason, the embroiderer who can turn her hand to a wide variety of methods will have the advantage of being able to choose from a wider range of design material. More ideas for treatment will suggest themselves to her, and she will be less easily thwarted by the prospect of seeing a wonderful design idea but lacking sufficient technical knowledge to be able to use it. This does not mean that an inexperienced needlewoman has no chance of creating a work of interest and beauty—on the contrary, she can work for a long time with a very limited repertoire of stitches. However, as she becomes more critical of her own and other people's work she will realize the dangers of not widening her technical horizons. Repeated colour schemes and subject matter are two other ruts all embroiderers tend to fall into unless they are aware of these dangers and try to avoid them. Many embroiderers do in fact specialize in one type of work, either by concentrating on one particular method like machine embroidery, goldwork or pulled thread, or by producing embroideries for a particular purpose as in church or dress embroidery. But these embroiderers do not restrict themselves because they know of no other way; they have reached this stage after many years of practice and experimentation, finally having attained their own high standard in one particular field as a result of personal choice and skill.

In this book I suggest ways of using some of the ancient designs illustrated, but entirely different treatments may occur to you when you look at them. This is good; it means that you are seeing the source material in terms of embroidery and that your interpretations will be unique. Ignore those who say that a circular design or one with flowing lines cannot be done on canvas—it can. Go ahead and do it. Forget the rule that you must only use one colour in Assisi work or that blackwork is always black. This is not so. Try to use fabrics and materials in new ways, not just for the sake of being different, but to make your design alive, interesting and personal.

There are many excellent books giving details of stitchery techniques, macramé, crochet, knitting and other textile forms (see Bibliography). This book offers design ideas, tells you how to look for them, and gives suggestions on how they may be used. Nevertheless here is a brief list of techniques which may encourage the beginner to widen her experience of interpretation, and suggest ways to the more experienced embroiderer which may not, at first, have occurred to her.

Assisi work

This is a form of cross stitch embroidery in which the stitches cover the background leaving the design area unworked. Single cross stitch is often used, although the stitches originally used for this type of work were long-armed cross and two-sided Italian cross. These two give a richer appearance to the work. Holbein and back stitch are used for outlining the motif. (See **7a** and **7b** below).

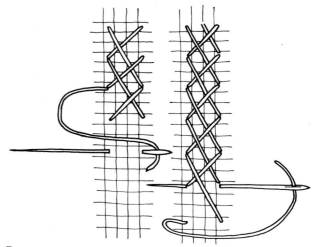

7a
Long armed Italian cross stitch.

14

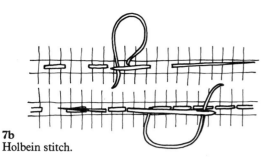

7b
Holbein stitch.

Particularly effective when the motif is used in silhouette form, some unusual effects can be obtained by the use of several shades and tints of the same colour.

Designs from Guatemalan and Mexican woven textiles are rich in ideas for Assisi work, as they are almost always in silhouette form on a white background. The delightful little figures, animals and plants, as well as the geometric designs, are perfect for embroiderers to adapt (see below).

Blackwork

This method can make use of counted or non-counted thread stitches, and of surface stitchery. It is usually worked in one predominant colour—black, brown or red—on white, with or without metal threads. Denser areas are achieved by the use of thicker thread, or by using more stitches placed closer together.

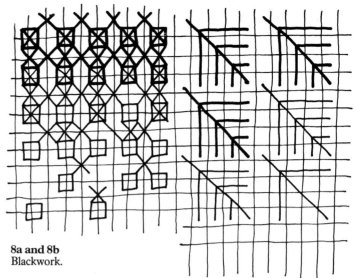

8a and 8b
Blackwork.

For stitch arrangements, look particularly at mosaic pavements from Greek, Byzantine and Roman sources, and for design ideas try cave paintings, Stone Age implements and ground marks (Chapter 11). These would all adapt well to this method because they can be expressed without the use of colour, and because they all require a large range of tonal values, which blackwork supplies admirably.

Canvas embroidery

Canvas or any fairly loosely woven evenweave fabric can be used, from the very finest to rug-making canvas. It is usual to cover the whole of the fabric with closely packed stitches, although unworked or partly worked areas may be left, as long as the effect obtained in this way forms part of the design. Much depends on the purpose, of course, as a stool top left partly unworked would wear unevenly.

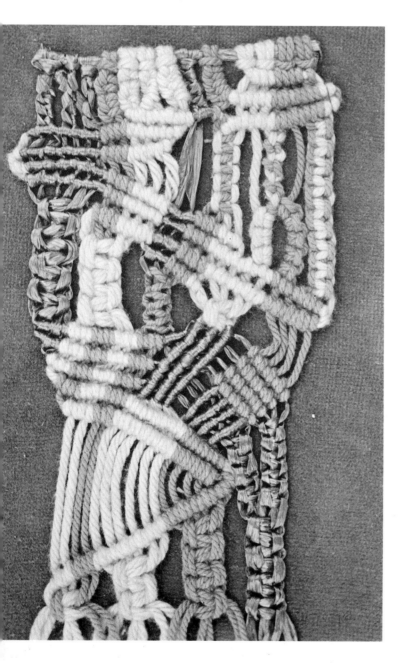

9

Macramé

The use of a variety of threads in macramé can produce effects different from the more usual symmetrical designs associated with this craft. Use was made in this sample of Anchor soft cotton, cotton macramé cord and Raffene (a synthetic raffia) and a very few of the simplest knots. The cords can be brought through a background fabric to create knots on the surface of a piece of work, before being used for stitches, thus combining macramé and embroidery on the same piece.

10

Knitted and crocheted three-dimensional group: spires

The bases of the spires are crocheted in popcorn stitch, (any large bobble stitch will have the same effect) then stitches were picked up on a knitting needle and knitted up to the top, decreasing at regular intervals. The shapes were then sewn up and slightly stuffed.

The background shows a knitted plaited cable and a crocheted border of 'fingers' with a single chain sewn down the opposite side. The round motif was made by crochet, increasing into a flat spiral with a mohair yarn.

11

Opposite

Raised leaf-like shapes in a group

Crocheted shapes like this are made by increasing into every stitch on every row starting with a chain of about six. This increase of stitches overcrowds and buckles, forming a firm leaf-like shape. In between these are small rolls of felt and a scattering of french knots.

This type of embroidery is often erroneously referred to as 'tapestry work'. Tapestry is, in fact, a form of weaving done on a loom, where the weft is beaten down hard to hide the warp completely. Canvas embroidery is pure stitchery, and many different textures are used in its composition. Many yarns and threads may be used as long as they do not distort the fabric as they pass through it. Try using silks and cottons as well as wools, raffia, string and natural fibres, and combine canvas stitches with other surface stitches not normally associated with this method. Pulled thread stitches can also be used on some types of canvas, and design ideas need not be limited to those made up of rigid geometrical shapes, through small irregularly shaped areas are difficult to cover.

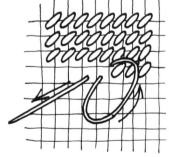

12
Canvas work.

Pulled work

Fabrics which are fairly evenly and loosely woven are necessary for pulled work, in which the warp and weft threads are not removed but pulled together, or apart, by stitches. This forms patterns of stitchery with varying densities and open areas. Pulled work looks best when the sewing thread is the same colour as the fabric, though it may be of varying thickness and quality, so that the stitches

and holes produce an overall texture rather than a series of differently coloured areas.

This is a very attractive way of filling in solid shapes, even small and irregular ones, and creating interesting and delicate textural effects, especially if used with padded or quilted areas or a low-pile tufting stitch. Gold thread may be used as the sewing thread, where suitable, to give a rich and sparkling effect.

African carvings (see Chapter 12) are rich in ideas suitable for this method; many of the carvings are profusely covered with patterned shapes which lend themselves perfectly to this kind of interpretation.

Drawn thread work

Hedebo, Hardanger and Russian drawn ground are all types of drawn thread embroidery; in this technique threads are withdrawn from the fabric so that vertical or horizontal threads are left upon which to embroider by grouping, darning and interlacing. It is usual to work with threads of the same colour as the fabric, as the technique relies for its effectiveness on the arrangement of holes and lacy stitches rather than on colour.

The angular and step formation of the designs on the blankets of Arabia and North America (see Chapter 12) are suitable for adaptation into drawn thread embroidery, as are the geometric designs seen on twined baskets and the woven and plaited mats produced in many countries.

13
South American Llama motif; this design is suitable for pulled thread work.

14a
Drawn thread work. Weaving the ends
of the threads back into the fabric.

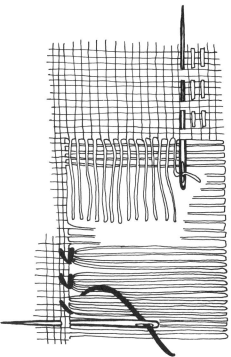

14b
Gathering threads with an overcast stitch.

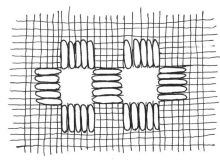

14c
Kloster blocks used to outline a square hole in Hardanger
embroidery.

Needleweaving

Like drawn thread embroidery, needleweaving is
worked on one set of threads only—either the warp
or the weft of the fabric—the other set having been
withdrawn. The threads are woven upon with
threads of the same colour or a contrasting one
forming a design. Nowadays a much freer interpretation of this method allows a greater range of
textured threads to be used with added warp.

In recent years, needleweaving has broadened in
concept towards what is known as 'off-loom weaving'.

This involves the use of any structure which will
hold warp threads taut—hoops, frames, branches
or other objects, which will then form part of the
finished piece. A background fabric is not necessary
here, since the embroiderer creates woven areas
and spaces where she requires them, to build up her
own motif. Found objects and some of the knotting
and wrapping techniques are often used, as well as
pompoms and tassels.

15a
Motif based on the Australian X-Ray fish.

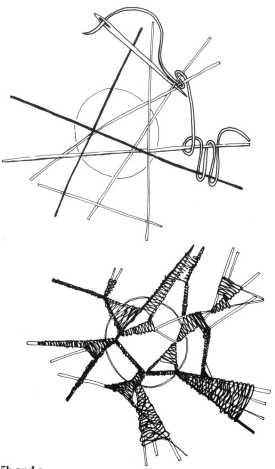

15b and c
Needleweaving. Holding down a piece of shisha glass with
needleweaving.

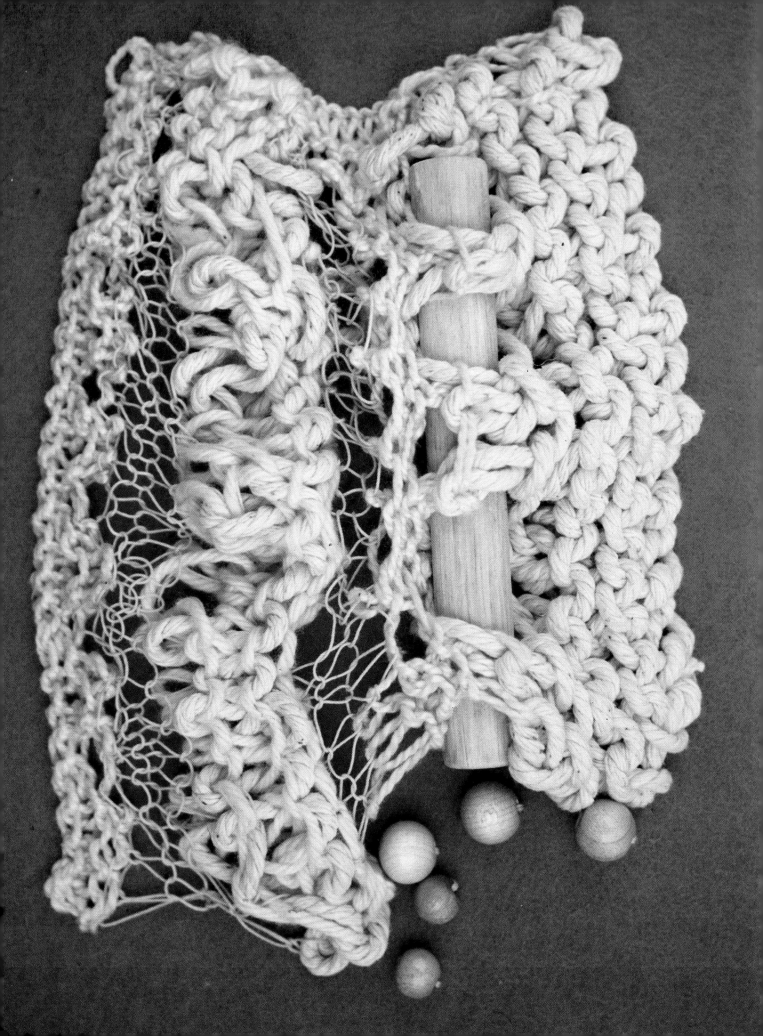

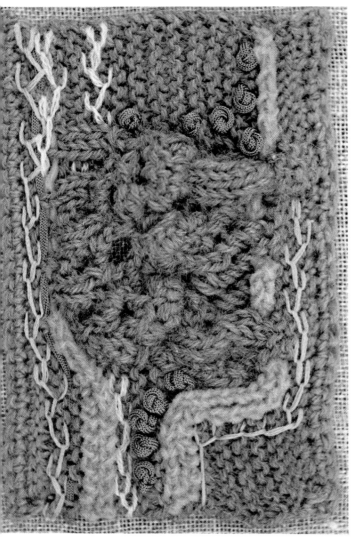

17

Above

Knitting—rectangular piece

Viewed with the sides at top and bottom this sample of knitting looks like a complicated series of stitches, yet is merely cabling at random with holes made here and there. The two lighter lines at the sides are separate pieces of ribbing in chenille sewn on afterwards, with bright yellow feather stitch alongside.

16

Opposite

String knitting

Interesting textured areas can also be made by knitting strings of various thicknesses, especially if the knitting needles used are of widely differing thicknesses too.

The needles used for this sample were numbers 3 and 10, with fine crochet cotton, medium and very thick string, producing a variety of lacy holes, some of which were made in the usual way by knitting two stitches together and making one. Stitches can also be easily picked up from one edge and knitted along in a different direction, as has been done here along the top.

18

Above

Crochet—oval piece with rings

Crocheted in red wool, this sample shows how an exciting area of texture can be made by the use of bobble stitches and open spaces between trebles. Crochet can be continued from a cast-off knitted edge shown by the small triangle of knitting in the lower half of the sample, and also from side edges to effect a change of direction. The buttonhole rings were made over small plastic curtain rings, then sewn on to the background.

All samples measure approximately 6 × 4½ in. (15 × 11.5 cm.).

Other off-loom weaving techniques

These include those methods of weaving which use the weaver and another stationary object to keep the warp threads taut between them.

The back-strap loom was used the world over by the earliest weavers, and is still used in many countries today to produce some of the finest and most beautiful fabrics.

Tablet weaving also uses the back-strap method, through here the warp threads pass through holes in a set of cards or 'tablets' which control the spaces through which the weft passes. We know that this is an ancient form of weaving, as a set of fifty-two tablets was found in a burial ship at Oseberg in Norway, set up ready for use on a loom. The method was also known and used in other parts of Scandinavia as well as in ancient Egypt and China.

Braiding and finger-weaving too, are ancient techniques which can be used to good effect, either in conjunction with stitchery or with the other twining and knotting techniques — macramé and knitting. These methods produce narrow strips of fabric which can be sewn together to make wider pieces if required.

Sprang, twining, netting and macramé

These are all ways of intertwining threads to produce decorative and mesh-like fabrics, which have been made all over the world for thousands of years. The interlaced knot designs of Celtic art tell us that the twining technique of these ancient people was highly developed. In other countries, ancient *and* primitive people have produced work of an extremely high standard using these methods. The Greeks and Vikings made their snoods (hair nets) using netting and sprang; sometimes they used metal threads and inserted small jewels here and there.

Macramé is a particularly apt technique for some of the design ideas in this book, as it is a textile art which originated in earliest history. Examples have been found from ancient Egypt and Arabia — the name in fact derives from an Arabic word. Macramé enthusiasts find inspiration in ancient and primitive jewelry, especially pendants, but masks and many other objects are also a source for design ideas.

19a
Macramé. A motif taken from a Persian textile, covered with tassels and fringes it is a good subject for different macramé knots.

Knitting and crochet

As the arts of knitting and crochet are both very ancient, it is worthwhile to experiment and explore their possibilities in relation to design ideas from ancient and primitive art, either in conjunction with stitchery or on their own. Hairpin and Tunisian crochet, French knitting and tatting can also be used in new ways to achieve rich and exciting textural effects. Small primitive motifs, especially those of a geometric nature are easy to knit into a garment; sculptural objects can be knitted and crochet to hang with beads, bells and tassels; and lacy-textured knitted or crocheted fabric will provide an interesting background for other methods such as appliqué or needleweaving.

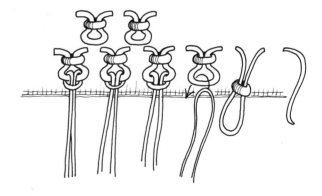

19b
Bringing threads from the background of a piece of embroidery, threading them through beads and using macramé knots.

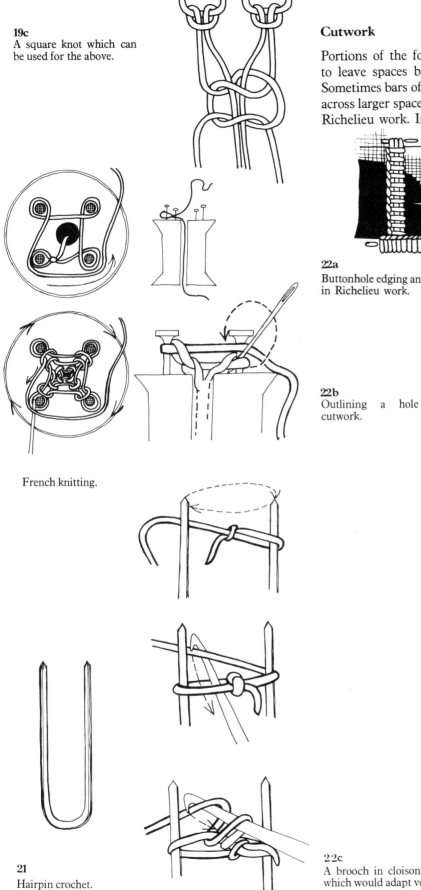

19c
A square knot which can be used for the above.

French knitting.

21
Hairpin crochet.

Cutwork

Portions of the foundation material are cut away to leave spaces between and around the motifs. Sometimes bars of lace-like embroidery are worked across larger spaces, as in Renaissance cutwork and Richelieu work. In reticella cutwork the design is

22a
Buttonhole edging and bar in Richelieu work.

22b
Outlining a hole for cutwork.

22c
A brooch in cloisonné enamelling made by the Visigoths which would adapt very well to a design in cutwork.

23

formed entirely by stitches across an open space, which form a lace-like fabric.

For ideas, look carefully at carvings, reliefs and sculptures which use negative spaces, such as the openwork wood carvings of Melanesia (see Chapter 12) and those of the Vikings (see Chapter 11), and at pictures of jewelry which often suggest arrangements for cut-away areas and linking stitchery.

Shadow work

This is worked on a transparent material in such a way that the reverse of the stitch shows through on to the right side.

Delicate motifs taken from ancient jewelry are adaptable for this technique, as are patterned animals and birds, decorative lettering and symbols (see Chapter 13).

Smocking

This technique is most often used nowadays as an ornament for children's clothes. In fact, it can also be used successfully on some of the more unusual fabrics to create interesting areas of pattern and texture, not always in the regular rows which have traditionally characterized it, but in a much freer way. Wool and fancy threads can be used, and beads and jewels will highlight particular areas.

Smocking can be used when designing from draperies, as it controls fullness in a highly decorative way.

24
Smocking. Folds seen on a Greek statue suggest interesting ideas for smocking.

Surface stitchery

This is a general term given to stitches which decorate the surface of the fabric by going in and out of it in the usual way. The important thing to remember is that one stitch can make a number of entirely different statements if it employs a variety of threads. The scope for design ideas in ancient and primitive art is enormous, but do try to find new ways of using surface stitches for your ideas by constant experimentation, so that your treatment is quite individual and unique.

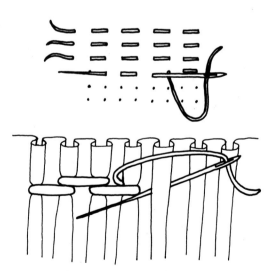

23
Smocking.

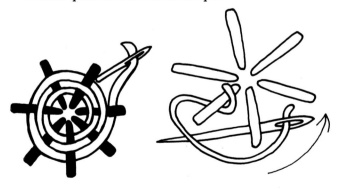

25
Surface stitches forming spider's web patterns.

Monochrome embroidery, though not a separate technique, must not be forgotten, since the idea of using one colour has much to recommend it. White threads of various weights and qualities on a white fabric create a subtle and pleasing effect, especially when part of the design is expressed by a method which alters the structure of the fabric—for instance pulled work or needleweaving.

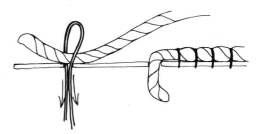

26b
Using a Chenille sling to take the end of the couched thread down to the underside of the fabric.

Couching

Couched threads are laid on the surface of the material and held down with another thread which either remains invisible, or can be made obvious to form part of the design.

This is a particularly useful method of using yarns and textured fibres which cannot easily be pulled through the background fabric. It looks well on linear designs, for outlining or emphasizing an interesting shape, for filling in areas of design, and in conjunction with almost any other technique. Beware of letting a couching thread meander about without any real purpose simply because nothing else springs to mind. Used with intent, a line of couching can provide just the right finishing touch to a piece of work; be bold, but careful!

26c
Pattern for couching from a detail of a carved grave post made by Australian Aborigines.

Appliqué

This is a method of applying one fabric to another with hand or machine stitchery, either decorative or invisible.

There are various methods of working appliqué, such as hemmed or unhemmed, inlay, padded and reverse. In reverse appliqué, shapes are cut out of a piece of fabric which is then placed over a second, different piece, so that the underneath layer shows through the holes. The raw edges are turned under and stitched down, unless the fabric is of a non-fraying kind, such as felt. For unusual effects in appliqué try using PVC, leather and suede, plastic, netting from vegetable bags, curtain netting and knitted fabrics.

A large variety of design sources exists for this type of embroidery. Look especially for shapes which are not too intricate: bold designs, like those on the pottery of the north-west American Indians

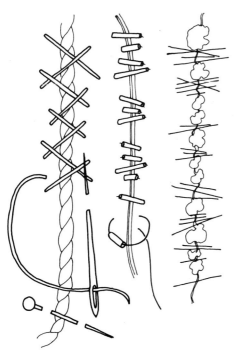

26a
Couching. Various ways of couching using herringbone stitch, beads and straight stitches.

25

(see Chapter 12), would adapt very well. In addition to its use as the main theme of an embroidery, appliqué can be used to complement other techniques, and it is often seen with surface stitchery and couching. For a change, try combining simple appliqué with cutwork, reverse appliqué and padded quilting to achieve a truly built-up, three-dimensional effect.

Patchwork

In patchwork, small shapes of material, usually cut from a template, are joined together to make one complete piece of fabric. Any shapes can be used so long as they fit together perfectly.

Design ideas can be found on mosaic and tiled floors, and in the brickwork of ancient and primitive buildings, for instance in Inca temples in Peru; also in the woven bags of American Indians and the woven pile-cloths of Central Africa. Designs for patchwork need not be rigidly geometrical, of course; much depends on the skill and ingenuity of the embroiderer.

In clothing and household textiles, the same type of fabric should be used throughout a piece of patchwork, to avoid stress and wear. However, patchwork for purely decorative purposes can include more unusual fabrics and be combined with other methods. Patchwork wall hangings can be combined effectively with needleweaving, quilting, surface stitchery, drawn and pulled thread work, and many other techniques.

Quilting

There are four main types of quilting—wadded, flat, corded and stuffed—and they can be used either separately or together. They can be worked either by hand or machine, and can also be combined with other methods of embroidery, for example pulled work, gold work and canvas embroidery. Knitted and crocheted shapes can also be quilted, if the knitted fabric is first lined to prevent the padding from escaping.

Ancient coins and seals (see Chapter 11) provide beautiful design ideas, since the surfaces are in relief and intaglio, often with a textured or patterned area too. Linear designs like the interlaced Celtic and Viking sculptures and wood carvings are sources of inspiration for corded quilting. Indeed, some form of padding or quilting is sometimes quite irresistible on a piece of work no matter what the origin of the design idea, for the technique is one which lends itself to a wide variety of interpretations.

26

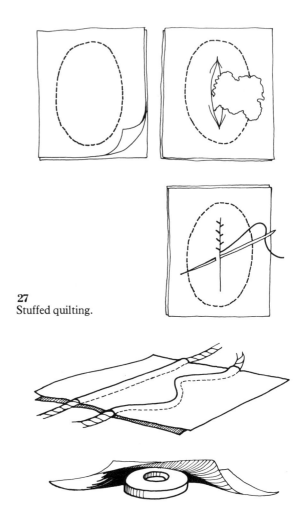

27
Stuffed quilting.

28
Padding with string and corn plaster.

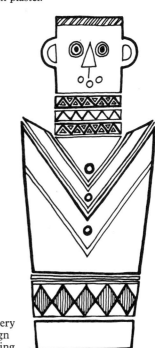

29
A piece of earthenware pottery from Czechoslovakia, a design suitable for all kinds of quilting.

Machine embroidery

In recent years, the important role of the sewing machine in the creation of embroidery has been finally recognized. Every embroiderer should acquaint herself with her machine's capabilities in order to use it to best advantage, since apart from creating beautiful and unusual effects in stitchery, quilting, appliqué and 'finishing' jobs can be done quickly and efficiently.

There is such a wealth of material available to anyone designing for machine embroidery that I can think of few designs which even a basic sewing machine would not be able to execute, either in pure stitching or in one of the other techniques such as appliqué, quilting or couching.

Metal thread embroidery

Gold has been used in embroidery from earliest times since man realized its beauty and made it a symbol of life-giving power. Samples of gold and silver thread have been found in textiles in the ancient graves of Sweden and Norway, and the gold of Byzantine ecclesiastical embroidery is well known.

The effect of gold thread when used on designs of ancient origin is remarkably appropriate; the monochrome yet sumptuous appearance strongly expresses the finely carved reliefs of ancient Egypt and Assyria (see Chapter 11), and yet can be used on a primitive geometrical design in a completely different way—with stunning effect.

Rug-making methods

I include these techniques because they create areas of texture which can be very useful in embroidery, as well as being crafts in their own right. The methods, and choice of background fabrics, are many and varied: it is worthwhile investigating them to find out their advantages and limitations. Rug canvas will take many unusual fibres; those illustrated include rug thrums, Turkey rug wool, handspun sheep's wool, raffia, strips of chamois leather and unspun flax, fleece and synthetic fibres. Patches of animal fur have been stuck on to the canvas, blending successfully with the other fibres. Interesting contrasts in texture can be obtained by combining rug-making techniques with padded leather areas.

The study of ancient, and particularly primitive, art will provide many ideas for using rug-making methods, but beware of trying to express tiny motifs in a long-pile technique as their shapes may easily become lost.

Three-dimensional embroidery

Three-dimensional embroidery is not so much a technique as a concept which can be expressed in a variety of ways, either for the purpose of lending extra interest to a piece of flat work, or to create an entirely free-standing or hanging object.

Techniques which lend themselves particularly well to this type of work are knitting and crochet, macramé, weaving and rug-making methods, and canvas embroidery. Stumpwork, raised work, high padding and quilting are among some methods of creating a protruding area of interest from an otherwise flat surface, as is a highly textured area such as a shaggy pile or tufting. Pieces of moulded polystyrene (the kind sometimes used for packing purposes), and cardboard tubing are useful as light-weight bases for three-dimensional work.

dresses. The nomads of the Sahara Desert create a brilliant effect on their camel and horse-trappings with pompoms and tassels which toss and bounce with the movement of the animal.

Features like these add an extra dimension to embroidery if used with discrimination ·and taste, and a certain amount of primitive exuberance when used with knitting, macramé and the other knotting and weaving methods (see Frontispiece). They also add originality to dress embroidery on collars, belts and edgings, fastenings and hood-tassels.

For ancient sources, see the friezes of Assyrian soldiers and their tasselled horses, and Egyptian figures wearing ornate collars, pendants, tasselled belts and sashes (Chapter 11).

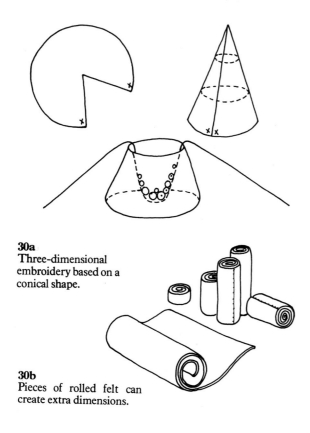

30a
Three-dimensional embroidery based on a conical shape.

30b
Pieces of rolled felt can create extra dimensions.

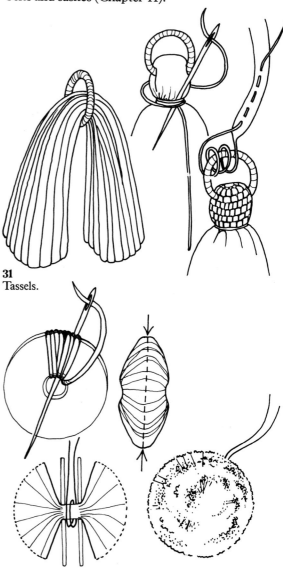

31
Tassels.

32
Pom-poms.

Tassels, pompoms and fringes

A walk round any museum of ethnography will show that tassels, pompoms, fringes and similar decorations occur extensively in primitive art. Clothes are bedecked with beads, wrapped fringes, shells and feathers. American Indians make extensive use of tassels and fringes on tunic sleeves, shoulder-seams and trousers, slippers and head-

5 About primitive designs

The term 'primitive' in art extends from the Stone Age to the present day cultures of the native races of Africa, the South Seas, America and certain parts of Asia.

In recent years, collectors and designers have begun to appreciate the beauty of these designs and to give them their proper places in the world of art, and as a result of this interest we can now see the work of primitive societies at first hand in museums and art galleries. Their art should not be seen merely as a series of fumbling and unsuccessful attempts at artistic expression, but as beautiful, spontaneous and uncomplicated work, often linked with religion and magic.

Because of our modern tendency towards unification in art, many of these designs could be adapted by the most discriminating of designers in fashion, jewelry, interior decoration and textiles, and particularly in fabric printing, rug-making, weaving and embroidery.

This Ba Pende African mask is the kind of object to stimulate the embroiderer's imagination, producing many different ideas for design, both abstract and figurative.

6 Where to look

When searching for design material from historical and primitive sources you will not only find the most exciting material and see it in a new light as potential embroidery, but also learn much about the history of the world, and of its art, both ancient and modern. For although some ancient art is primitive, there are still primitive societies today which produce work of great beauty.

Few of us are lucky enough to be able to travel around the world's museums, or to see at first hand the work of primitive people, but nevertheless a wealth of material can be found in museums nearer home, and your library should contain illustrated books on the subject. Your local museum probably has flints and axe-heads, Celtic and Anglo-Saxon jewelry, coins, ceramics, cutlery and domestic equipment. In a museum you can judge for yourself the colour, texture and scale of the article, uninfluenced by photographic reproduction, and often a completely new light is shed on an object seen in this way.

Many curators of museums are quite willing, on request, to remove articles from a showcase for you to see and sketch. Most museums sell postcards of their exhibits, and these are worth collecting. All designers benefit from keeping both a sketchbook and a scrapbook of design ideas. Look out for pictures of ancient and primitive art, and keep them together in your scrapbook for easy reference. Take your sketchbook in a bag or pocket, wherever you go, and note down any ideas which you see. Do not feel self-conscious when you are sketching; many people draw nowadays, both in museums and outside. I find that people rarely take notice or see anything unusual in it. Some of the larger museums provide sketch boards for anyone wishing to sketch or make notes. Ask at the reception desk.

Your sketches may seem crude and hesitant at first, but as long as they remind *you* of the design you have seen then that is all that matters. Use pencils, charcoal, pastel or wax crayons. Do not attempt to make a polished and detailed study; just a rough idea of the main essentials will do, with perhaps a very small area of detail to remind you. If, for instance, you are particularly impressed by a tiny design round the base of a vase, leave the shape of the vase to your memory and just sketch the design briefly, making a note of the colours and any other factors which are important to you. Always make a note of the design source, its date, the number of the showcase and the name of the museum; then if you should want to find it again later you will be able to do so much more easily. Try to look at the objects with greater perception than you may have done before, bearing in mind the possible translation of a detail into embroidery. Do not walk past the case of Stone Age flints; look at them carefully and note their cleverly hewn surfaces, see how the light catches on some facets and how others are thrown into shadow. Would that make a good background treatment for a piece of canvas embroidery? Try to see shapes and shadows in the negative spaces too, and in the way objects are arranged inside a showcase.

Books of all kinds are valuable sources of material: look in your local library for children's reference and history books, books about ancient civilizations and their art, history and pre-history and the study of primitive people. Remember that 'art' includes the whole range of creative forms—wood carving, sculpture, textiles, in fact anything which has led Man to express himself visually.

33
This design of a Roman iron cooking-grid is strongly reminiscent of a patchwork cushion.

Embroiderers can find a wealth of design ideas in exhibitions such as this one on Yoruba Religious Cults held recently at the Museum of Mankind in London. The picture shows a reconstruction of the Shango shrine.

7 How to look

It is important to remember that whenever you find a source of inspiration, it is *design* you are looking for and not something to copy or imitate as closely and as representationally as possible. Embroidery is, after all, a design medium, and it should not strive to copy any man-made or natural object *as it has already been presented* in its original medium in all its exact detail. The embroiderer must choose which element of her inspirational source she wishes to use and then work out her design in her own style with her own characteristic stamp upon it, so that it becomes an embroidery of her own personal design based on an idea which may have been presented by someone else, but in a different form, many thousands of years ago. A design from a Roman mosaic pavement may be exactly what she wants to use on a cushion, but it will not look like a mosaic floor when she has interpreted it in her way—it will look like an embroidered border. Similarly a design in padded chamois leather on a pendant may *remind* you of a Greek coin, but could not possibly be mistaken for the real thing as it is so obviously an embroidered design based on that idea, and not an exact copy of it. That the finished product does not actually look like the original source of inspiration does not matter at all. You can alter the design source in any way to please your own sense of design; you can combine ideas, repeat them, simplify them, or elaborate on them, so long as the source of inspiration helps you in designing. The finished piece of work must first be recognizable as essentially embroidery, or any creation in fabric or thread, and in your own style.

I do not recommend tracing a historical design from a book and using it just as it is: so much is lost from the original by tracing. It becomes less pure in line, and the lines round the edges of the photograph or drawing may not necessarily be the ones which will create the best design for embroidery. Look instead at the inspirational source as a whole, and try to decide what it is that appeals to you. Is it the delicacy of flowing rounded lines

within the object? Is it the clear-cut geometrical pattern? Or maybe it is the general distribution of light and shade within beautiful shapes? You may have many reasons for wanting to use that idea, but it helps to try to analyse its attractions for you. In this way, those parts of the design which are important to you will be emphasized, and the parts which are extraneous to your mental design can be blocked out. It is often helpful to look at an object through half-closed eyes, thus shutting out the details and seeing only the main lines, the general distribution of shapes, areas of dark and light, and colours fusing softly into each other. This is a particularly good way of looking at cave paintings which are sometimes crowded with detail and yet so very beautiful in their overall effect. Of course, some of the detail can be included after you have decided on the general impression you want to convey.

Try to look at potential designs for embroidery as fabric and thread, even if it is only a very small area—perhaps an interesting texture, shape, line, three-dimensional area, or a cluster of spangles. Make a mental note, or, better still, a sketch, however rough, to remind you.

The 'window' or 'viewer' method is popular with embroiderers for capturing a small detail and isolating it. Cut a square or round shape out of a piece of card. Place the card over the photograph or drawing which inspires you and capture part of it in your window. Move it around, looking carefully with half-closed eyes at the design possibilities in each portion of the picture. Try to visualize it as embroidery. Interpret textures as stitches, and areas as fabric. Try seeing it in a variety of techniques. Note which shapes you would like to keep or emphasize, and which ones disappear. Think how it could best be interpreted, bearing in mind its characteristics—its lines, textures and shapes.

Much depends on the purpose of the intended embroidery, although, as I have previously explained, a piece of embroidery is often done merely as an exercise in pure creative enjoyment. If you want a design for a specific purpose and technique, you must be quite sure that it is possible to use your design in this way to full advantage. If the purpose you have in mind will not happily 'marry' with the design idea—either because of the sheer impracticality of it, or because the technique you wanted to use will not be seen clearly, then you must either change your design, or your purpose, or the technique. A design which looks good in blackwork may not necessarily work as well in needleweaving, though it may work in other counted thread methods.

Remember that your embroidery does not have to represent any particular object, therefore colour need not be a problem. Many historical and primitive designs appeal to us because of their colour combinations, so if you want to retain this in your embroidery, then you should do so. If, on the other hand, you have a different colour scheme in mind there is no reason why it cannot be used, even to the extent of reducing all colour to black, white and all the shades of grey in between. But do think carefully about this, and ask yourself whether, by changing the colour combinations, you may lose some essential part of the original design. Does the colour scheme you have in mind still bring out the best in the design? Are the tonal values the same? Can you tone them down, or can you exaggerate them and make them more exciting? Or can you more successfully dispense with colour altogether and thereby create a design with textures, as in monochrome work or pulled thread embroidery? Your design for embroidery is not a representational picture—leaves need not be green, hair and fur need not be their natural colours, and the sun need not be red or yellow. Use colour to enhance your design, not to create solid, shaded, naturalistic shapes, but in a stylized and decorative way. This is the role of embroidery in design; the exciting combination of colour and texture in fabric and thread cannot be expressed in the same way in any other medium.

If people mistake your embroidered stylized African lizard for a pink crocodile, it may well be that they are not familiar with primitive art, but if the design is pleasing and the work is well executed, and if it gave you pleasure to make it, then the object of the exercise has been achieved.

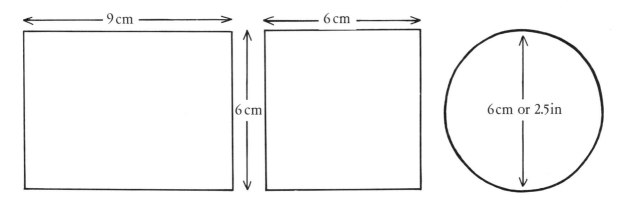

34
Take several sheets of paper or card, and cut out one of these shapes from the centre of each. Several sizes can be made.

8 Some ways of making a design

(1) Make a straightforward decorative rendering by reducing a motif down to its simplest possible two dimensional form, and then treating it in a decorative way suitable for an embroidery technique. (See **35** and **36**).

(2) Use a detail (part of a design or texture from an object), ignoring its environment and taking it completely out of context. (See **37**).

(3) Make a silhouette of an object suitable for interpretation into a solid shape. This can be cut and rearranged, perhaps in a series of lines complementing each other. (See **38**).

(4) Design from a shadow—shadows cast by objects and carvings—particularly ancient jewelry and glass through which light shines—are full of design potential. (See **39**).

(5) Design with negative shapes made by spaces between positive shapes. (See **40**).

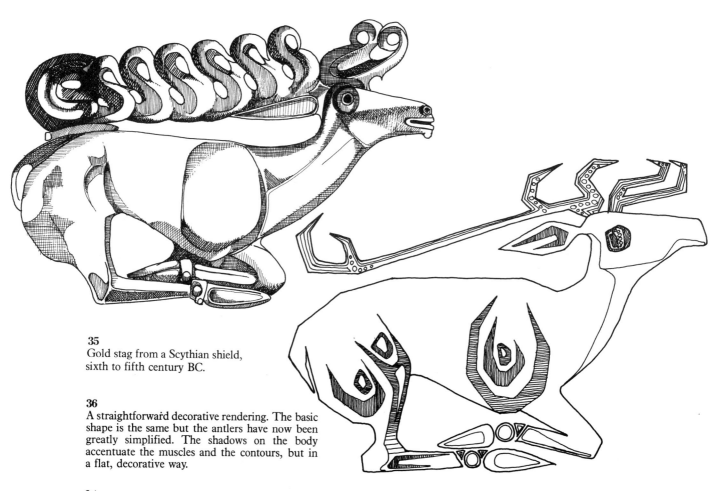

35
Gold stag from a Scythian shield, sixth to fifth century BC.

36
A straightforward decorative rendering. The basic shape is the same but the antlers have now been greatly simplified. The shadows on the body accentuate the muscles and the contours, but in a flat, decorative way.

34

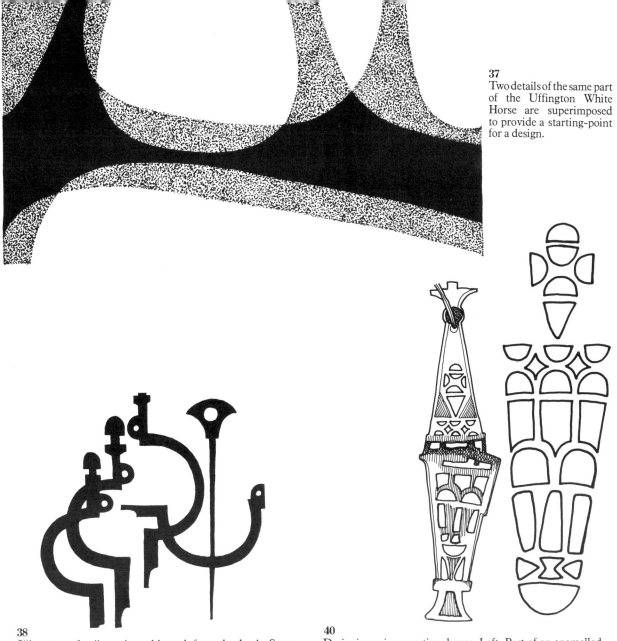

38
Silhouettes of a silver pin and brooch from the Anglo-Saxon period in England (AD 410-1066).

40
Designing using negative shapes. Left: Part of an enamelled pendant from central Russia. Fourth century AD. Right: The negative shapes, slightly rearranged to miss out the central area which served no purpose in the design. This type of design has many applications: e.g. quilting, padding, inlay and cutwork.

39
Here the whole shape has a shadowy shape behind it which could be worked in a finer thread or fabric.

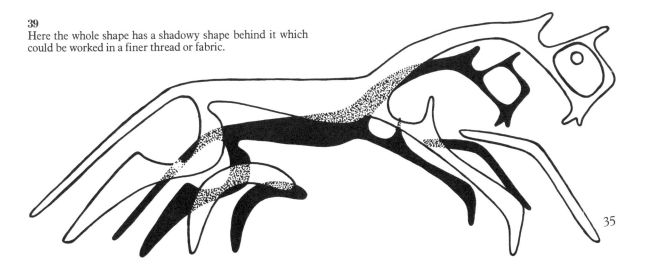

35

(6) For borders, cut motifs out of paper and place them end to end, upside-down, side by side; use a mirror to help you sort out the corners. For geometrical designs, try overlapping, reducing and enlarging parts, or isolating one motif from its usual background. (See **41**).

(7) Cut one motif into two or more sections and rearrange the pieces, or treat one half as positive and the other as negative.

(8) Make several drawings on tracing paper of motifs and designs you find interesting, and superimpose one on top of another. This produces some exciting results, particularly if the one underneath is of a textural nature. Try this with ground marks and with large illuminated letters as seen in medieval manuscripts. (See **44**).

(9) Superimpose a design drawn on tracing paper on to an arrangement of geometrical shapes cut out

of newspaper, coloured tissue paper, magazine pages or brown paper. Use them to build a suitable background for your main design. Do not cut the tracing paper design; leave it on a whole sheet so that the edges of the pieces underneath blend together softly.

(10) Place a motif against a background of patterned fabric such as printed curtain material or woven furnishing fabric. The pattern of the material can be used to form a background to the design in a variety of ways: by accentuating its shapes or lines with stitchery; by folding and pleating to move motifs closer together; by toning down a patterned fabric by placing layers of net over it.

Tie-dyed and batik cloth can also be used as a background, with the advantage that the colours can be chosen and arranged to suit your own requirements (see section, *Textiles*).

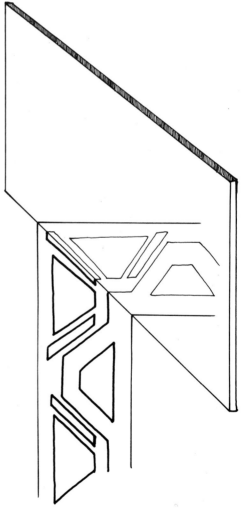

41
Motifs can sometimes be used in a circular arrangement too.

42
Place a mirror on its edge diagonally across the border and move it about until you find a satisfactory corner arrangement.

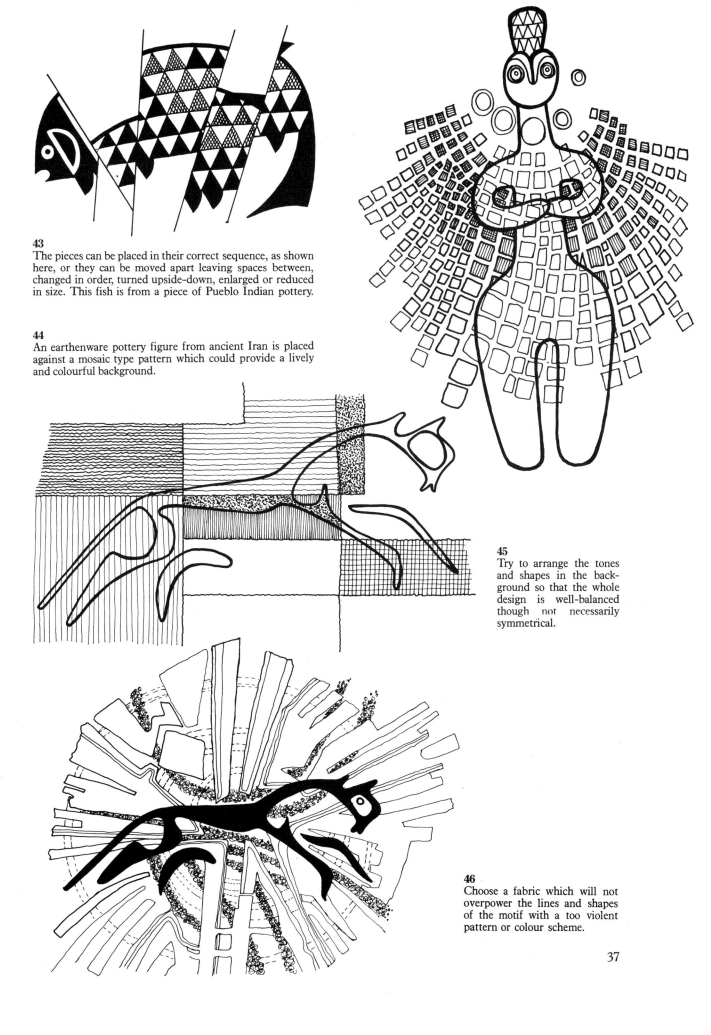

43
The pieces can be placed in their correct sequence, as shown here, or they can be moved apart leaving spaces between, changed in order, turned upside-down, enlarged or reduced in size. This fish is from a piece of Pueblo Indian pottery.

44
An earthenware pottery figure from ancient Iran is placed against a mosaic type pattern which could provide a lively and colourful background.

45
Try to arrange the tones and shapes in the background so that the whole design is well-balanced though not necessarily symmetrical.

46
Choose a fabric which will not overpower the lines and shapes of the motif with a too violent pattern or colour scheme.

(11) Combine a complete shape with a part (or parts) of that shape.

(12) Make an all-over pattern from one or more motifs.

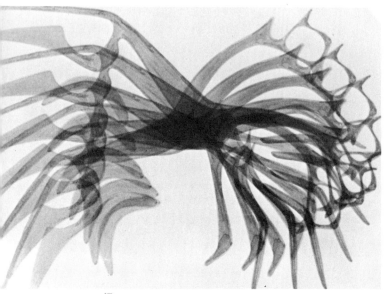

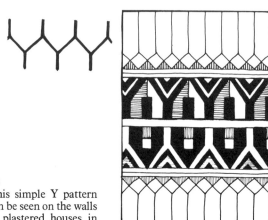

48
This simple Y pattern can be seen on the walls of plastered houses in some African villages.

47
Part or all of the resulting design may be used. Notice the interesting shapes made by the overlapping parts and by the spaces between.

49 Below
A camera enlarger or a projector can help make a design larger or smaller.

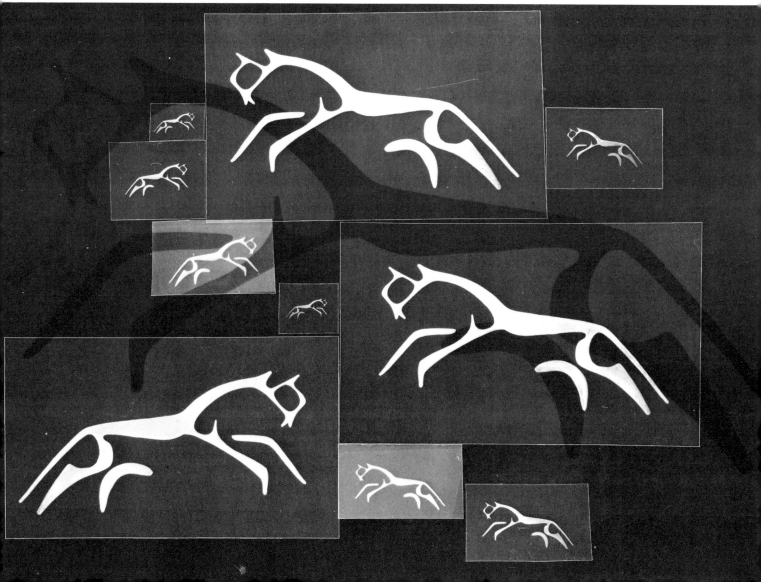

(13) Show multiple views of a subject in one design, for instance, profile and full-face of an animal or human being.

(14) Use the same motif in different sizes in one design, some overlapping.

(15) Alter the proportions of the subject, enlarging parts and reducing parts to focus attention on the more interesting shapes.

(16) Place a small detail of a design on a background which is an enlarged version of the same design. (See **53** below).

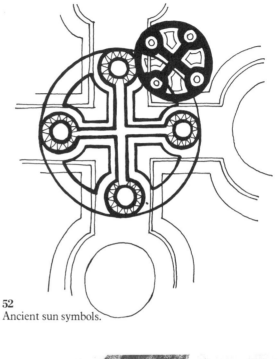

52
Ancient sun symbols.

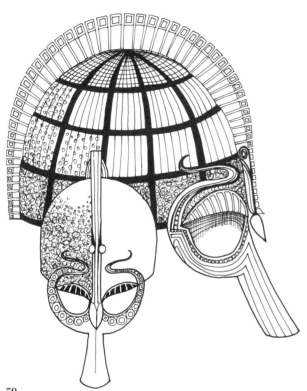

50
A seventh century bronze and iron helmet from the Vendel Graves in Sweden.

51
The carving on this Paumari Indian wooden club from Brazil has some beautiful shapes which are easily identified and enlarged.

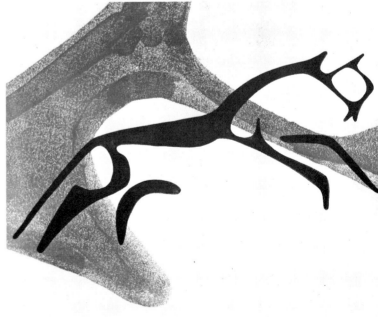

53
Here the background shape has been turned sideways to complement the flow of the motif.

(17) Interpret a design in a multiple linear fashion so that the edge or edges of the shape are repeated and enlarged, spacing the lines regularly or irregularly.

(18) Adapt and arrange a motif to fit inside a shape such as a circle, a square or a diamond.

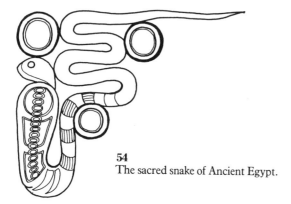

54
The sacred snake of Ancient Egypt.

55
String laid across the background can help to suggest the direction of stitches and related background shapes.

56
Loosely-woven fabric can be used effectively as a background when pulled into holes, frayed and distorted or used as a basis for pulled-thread work or needleweaving.

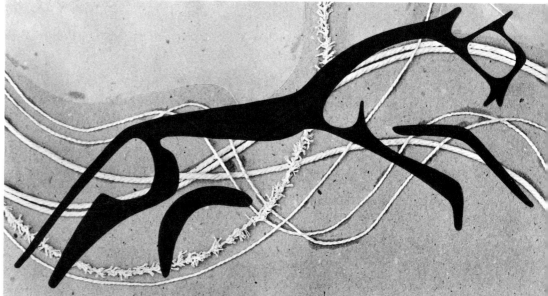

57
If strips are rearranged in different orders an exciting abstract design may result.

58
Cut a complete motif into very narrow strips then move them out of place, upwards and downwards. This creates a patchwork effect.

59
Furnishing fabrics offer a wide choice of designs and textures which can be used as backgrounds.

60
This bull's head motif can be used in a variety of ways, each one adapted to suit its own purpose. Though the basic layout remains the same, the foundation shapes are slightly changed to suit the dimensions and the technique. Primitive masks are useful sources of designs of this kind.

This panel could be worked in canvas embroidery with richly-textured threads, shisha glass, jewels and applied leather. There is also scope here for some padded areas, and the ring could hang loosely from the bull's nose. The background should be a well thought out part of the whole design, showing a colour and texture relationship to the main motif.

61
This four-sided arrangement of the bull's head motif makes the cushion look the same whichever way up it is placed. The main motif could be applied in a brilliant colour to a dull-coloured background of a different texture, and the details worked in heavy wools of black, white and the background colour. A sewing machine would help to fasten the main pieces down; a close zig-zag stitch could take the place of a hand embroidery stitch.

42

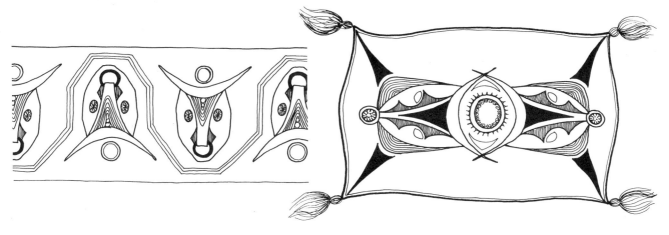

62

The same motifs can be used alternately upside-down and right-way-up to form a border design. The horns provide a pleasing undulating rhythm along the edges, and each motif fits the next like a jig-saw puzzle with the help of a line which could be of a colour already used in the background fabric.

63

Another cushion design shows the use of two motifs placed end to end. This, too, could be worked in appliqué, or entirely in machine embroidery with areas of stuffed and corded quilting. Notice how the tassels actually form part of the design.

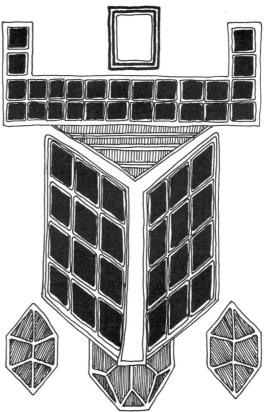

64

The two halves of this symmetrical motif are reversed; techniques such as reverse appliqué or blackwork could be used to good advantage here.

65

For a method such as pulled work or some cutwork methods the motif could be rendered entirely in straight lines, as in this simplified diagram. Many of the small details shown in the other diagrams would be unworkable here, and some details would become lost unless the design was enlarged enough to allow the pulled and stitched areas to have full effect.

9 Methods of designing

How to make a working drawing

The method used to create a working drawing from a source of inspiration depends on several factors, among them the simplicity (or complexity) of the desired design, the ability of the designer and the purpose of the intended embroidery.

I have already said that a straightforward tracing or copying, of a photograph from a book is not what designing is about. It is usually necessary or at least desirable to rearrange, remove or add to the material which inspires you. For this reason I would recommend the method which I use most often. I sit down with a large piece of paper, either white or coloured — depending on the tone of the overall idea in mind — and make a large number of fairly small rough sketches using those shapes and lines of the original idea which I want to include.

It is as well (though not essential) to have in mind right from the outset the method of embroidery you want to use, so that you can adapt the material to the limitations of that method. Some designs immediately suggest a method, and it is important not to ignore this and try to force the design into an alien technique which would not express the idea as well. Many designs are, of course, suitable for various interpretations, so keep an open mind when you begin sketching.

Do avoid the temptation to copy someone else's style, or use your design in exactly the same way you have seen it done before. Make plenty of small sketches based on your design source — whether it is a painting, a photograph, or a quick sketch you have made in a museum. Arrange your material in a variety of ways which will depend on the area you want to fill, the method of embroidery and its purpose. Intricate detail is not necessary at this stage, nor need the stitches be drawn in unless you are making several arrangements for different techniques, but even then only a suggestion is needed.

As far as you are able, gather together the materials you wish to use. These suggest ideas for treatment as you handle them and place them together.

Enlarging

Having decided on an idea, and the technique, and the purpose of the embroidery, you must now enlarge your chosen drawing to the actual working size. This can be done by the squared method.

66
Make sure that the measurements of the larger size are in the correct proportion to the smaller one. An error here could lead to distortion of the design.

Transferring the design

Lay the tracing paper on to your material, and after pinning down the corners, tack all the way round the edge to hold it firmly. Now tack with small stitches on the lines of the design through both the tracing paper and the background material. When this is done, gently pull away the paper, leaving the design outlined on the fabric.

This method of outlining is also used on canvas and larger backings for rugs and hangings, though in the latter case newspaper may be used instead of tracing paper. This is preferable to the prick and pounce method, as alterations to the design can be made simply by removing the tacked lines, whereas a painted line is more permanent. The tacking guidelines are removed, of course, as each part of the design is worked.

Designing without a working drawing

The design which has a definite outline and edge, and is divided into clearly defined areas of embroidery and space, presents few problems; you only need to draw the basic lines as boundaries in a certain arrangement. The other, less well-defined type of design relies more on textures or colours merging into each other, and has few, if any, clearly delineated edges. It is the kind of design which almost has to grow from one point and take its own course as the work progresses, although the end product is always firmly fixed in the mind's eye throughout the process.

In this case, one of the best ways of working is to collect up the fabrics and threads you want to use and lay them directly on to the background, cutting and pinning the fabrics, folding, tucking, pleating and 'scrunching' them, keeping in mind the areas of stitchery, looking now and again at the source of your inspiration to remind yourself of the ideas you wish to capture. Place the threads in bundles on the fabric to see if they will be suitable in colour and texture, and make a note of any other yarns you will need. Sort out other items you want to use, such as beads and jewels, but only if they will play a constructive part in the design. Begin by stitching down, in their correct position, any fabrics you want to use. Stitchery is usually added later.

Starting in this way, full of enthusiasm, is one of the most exciting methods of designing, as it produces results so quickly. However, although this method sounds free and easy, allowing much greater change of mind during the working process, it does in fact call for great discipline in order not to get carried away by too many ideas all at once. Remember that you do not want your embroidery to look like a sampler of stitches or a hotch-potch of fabrics with nothing to say. Keep in mind your original idea, and if in doubt, stop! Cover it up for a few days before turning to it again with fresh eyes. I find that it helps to hold it up before a mirror; this often reveals flaws in the arrangement which were not obvious before.

When designing for techniques like off-loom weaving, (weaving on a hoop or frame without a fabric background) or for macramé, crochet or knitted forms (see Chapter 4), it is usual to make a rough working drawing of the design and work straight from that. Once the design has been planned on paper, put away the original picture which inspired the design and only glance at it very occasionally (if at all) during the working process.

An exercise in interpretation

Occasionally you will see an interesting portion of design or texture which you are eager to interpret immediately into embroidery. This is the time for quick action; it is a challenge, a rewarding exercise, and one which forces the embroiderer to use imagination and skill. Miss out completely the drawing and planning stages; sort out differently textured yarns and fabrics too, if you need them, and start at once. There are no rules to follow here; just try to reproduce the texture or pattern of lines in stitches and fabric. You may find that the result will give you inspiration for a totally new piece of work.

This flowing design was derived from the carved brow and eyes of a Greek statue.

10 The case of the 'already perfect' design

Ancient and primitive art contains such an abundance of inspirational material that you may often see a wonderful idea which you simply cannot find a way of interpreting as embroidery. Sometimes the shapes of the original design are so perfect that there seems to be no way in which they can be adapted without at the same time spoiling them.

This particular difficulty presented itself when I was making the canvas embroidery of the three little figures from the cave wall, and when I designed the 'White Horse of Uffington' panels. The highly simplified shapes are so poetically delightful in concept that they need no alteration or embellishment. And so, at the risk of contradicting what I have previously said about not using a design in its original form, I feel that nevertheless there *are* special cases where there is no alternative.

I would suggest that if you meet such a case you should think about it for a long time before starting to work on it. You must decide whether, in fact, your interference in its proportions and design will make it more interesting, or whether by your suggested interpretation you will destroy what at first appealed to you. In the two cases mentioned, you can see that I decided to leave the shapes exactly as they were in the original, and to concentrate on the background; I felt that to attempt to alter the shapes in any way would be quite pointless, whereas the background was open to a variety of interpretations. If you are completely at a loss about the treatment of such a design, it is better to put it away for a time. It would be a far graver mistake to abuse it by insensitive treatment than not to use it at all.

Part II
Source material and inspiration

11 Ancient civilizations

Cave paintings

The earliest known examples of cave art, at Altamira in northern Spain, date from about 30,000 BC. Specimens of cave paintings have been discovered in areas as far apart as Scandinavia, Siberia, the Far East and America, but they are all of a later vintage. The aboriginals of Australia still paint on rocks in their timeless traditional style, depicting animals, hunters and religious legends.

Early Man drew with his fingers in the damp clay of cave walls; then he started using charcoal, and paint made from mud, wood ash and other natural pigments. Later on he scratched and carved with sharp bone tools, producing some entirely realistic, some highly stylized and some completely abstract designs.

67
A charging bison of the Ice Age; a rock painting from Altamira, Spain. Only the front portion is shown here to illustrate the interesting arrangement of darker areas. Remove the eye, and you have the basis of an abstract design which could perhaps be interpreted in a raised surface stitch. Or leave the eye as it is, and treat it in a purely stylized way.

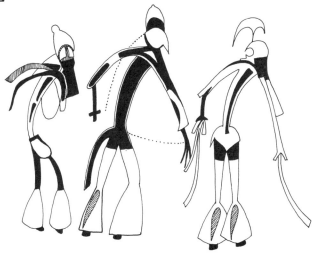

68
The figures are a small part of a group of dancers wearing masks and ornaments, from a cave wall in South Africa. The human body is rendered here in a highly symbolic manner, showing a beautiful rhythm of movement as the figures sway in the dance. The original painting was in dark brown and white on a rich red-brown background. The use of a lot of colour here would be quite unnecessary; it would probably detract from, rather than enhance, the forms and the spaces between them. Think of a method which would make best use of the lovely shapes, concentrating on form and texture rather than on colour.

69

Canvas embroidery of a prehistoric rock painting from Wadi Sera in Libya. The complete panel measures 9.2 × 7 in. (23 × 18 cm.). The three little figures creeping across the textured background have not been altered in any way except in size. The figures were first cut out of felt, then appliquéd on to shiny 'plastic leather', which in turn was appliquéd on to canvas previously prepared with tent stitch round the edges of the shapes. This was to help the needle make a firmer stitch on the canvas. The rest of the canvas was entirely covered with a mixture of tent stitch, French knots, square eyelets, diamond eyelets, and irregularly placed squares of diagonal stitches. The yarns used were 3- and 4-ply knitting wool, crewel wool, crochet cotton and stranded embroidery cotton. The roughness created on the background forms a complete contrast with the blank smoothness of the figures.

70

Drapery can be expressed very successfully using straight stitches, as can be seen on this sample of Florentine stitch on canvas. The flowing lines of drapery were worked without any previous preparation, mainly over two to five threads using double knitting wool, chenille, and lurex and wool, seen at the left of the sample. Worked by the author, the piece measures 3.9 × 5.1 in. (10 × 13 cm.).

48

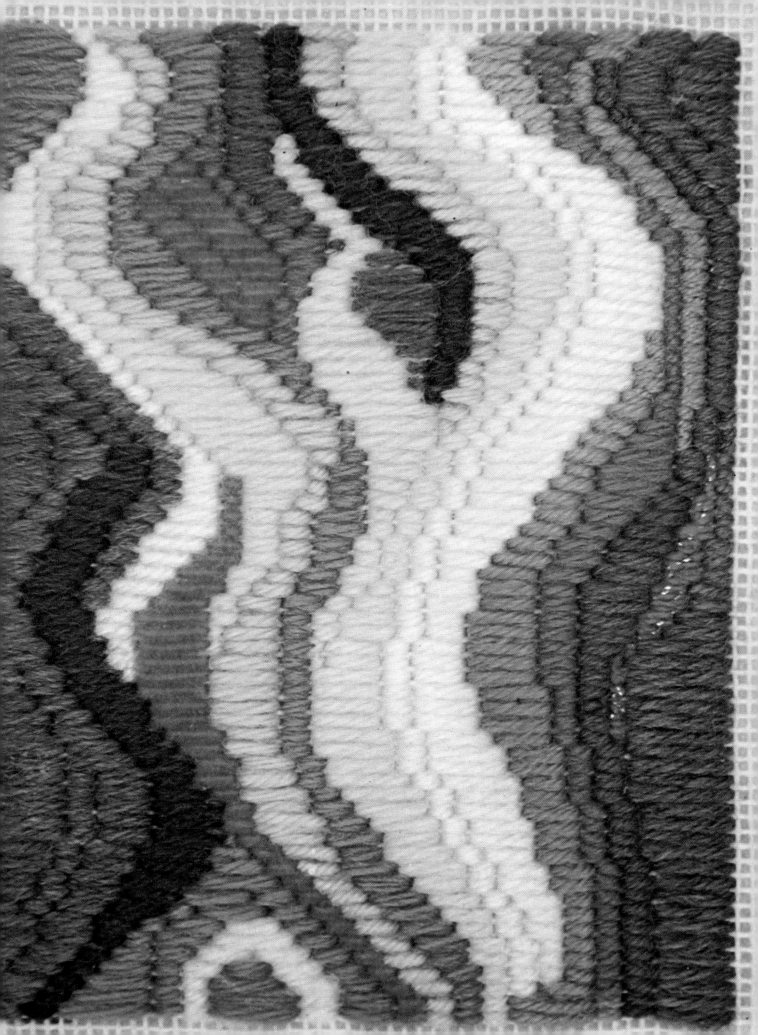

These delightful paintings and carvings are worth studying intently; their simplicity of form and economy of line could be a lesson to designers of embroidery—those early artists said what they *had* to say and no more. The colours at their disposal were few (they rarely used more than one colour with white to complete a painting), but how well they blend with the background rocks of red, yellow or brown sandstone, or grey and white limestone.

Ancient Egypt

The recent exhibition in Europe of the treasures of Tutankhamun has acquainted many people with the exquisite craftsmanship of Ancient Egyptian artists. We are fortunate to possess ample records of their daily lives, their deaths, their clothes, hairstyles, jewelry, furniture and gardens—everything, in fact, to give us a complete picture of these people. Consequently there is plenty of material for us to study, and no shortage of ideas to be acquired from all these sources. Even their tombs were works of art—how different from our own method of departure from this life!

72
This flower arrangement from a scene on the back of a chair was portrayed in beaten gold and enamels. I feel that it may be an example of the Egyptian artist's unorthodox sense of perspective, for example the round top part may, in fact, have been a flat tray on a stand, holding short flowers, with a central bunch of lotus blooms.

71
Sometimes a wealth of subject matter and detail makes it difficult for us to pick out one particular part on which to base our design. It takes practice to separate one part from another, and the 'window' method (see Chapter 7) is useful here. Try to break up a complicated design, such as this pectoral ornament, into different sections. The Egyptians certainly knew how to pack many motifs into one design without making it look in the least disjointed.

On the one hand, you may want to use the general shape of the object rather than the details.

73
Tombs were lavish affairs, with as much artistry spent on their decoration as on the palaces of the living. Hence some of the most beautiful wall paintings have been found there, like this one at Thebes of Queen Nefertari in whose tomb it was discovered.

If you cover up her face for a moment and ignore the tall head-dress, you can see the attractive arrangement of lines made by hat, hair and collar. Try to get this same kind of rhythm of complementary lines in your designs, not necessarily to fit inside a circle or any other shape but to relate them to each other and to make them play a useful part in the whole construction. If you find any lines without a particular role or purpose, eliminate them.

50

There is something in Egyptian art for every embroiderer, whether she is looking for symmetry or asymmetry, a border design, a colour scheme, a hanging shape, a square, circular or long pattern, figures, animals, plants, textures, symbolism or realism.

The Romans and Greeks

Being very much preoccupied with amassing wealth and collecting other people's countries, the Romans can hardly be said to have a unique art-style. Instead, they emulated that of the artistic Greeks not only in sculpture and architecture but also in fashion. Details can be found on which to base designs, particularly for dress embroidery, and textural effects based on hairstyles and costume.

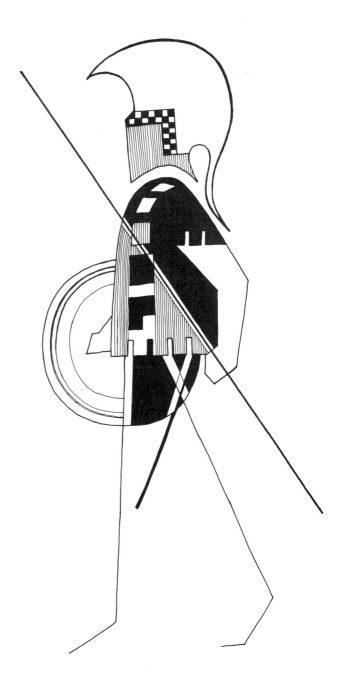

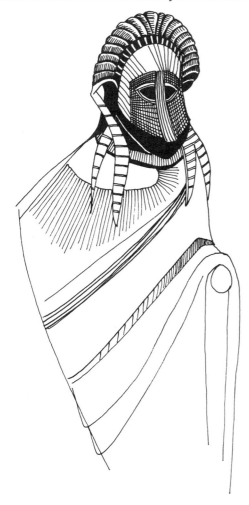

74

I found the shapes and shadows on the Spartan soldier's helmet (**75**) very interesting from an embroiderer's point of view. They suggest a variety of methods: quilting and padding, needleweaving, goldwork and machine embroidery —not necessarily all used together, of course. For ways of using a design like this, refer to Part 1 of this book.

75

Although recognizably a Roman or Greek soldier, this is purely a design of more or less geometric shapes and lines, with the interest centred on the upper part of the body.

In alternating the shading effects on the body, I discovered that an interesting patchwork pattern could be obtained by leaving some spaces empty, and although I had intended to continue the black shading on to the shield, I realized just in time that this might make the soldier look rather portly — which was not the impression I wanted to convey!

Had the main body part been heavier and more intricate, the lines in place of legs would have been rather inadequate. As it is, they are enough to help the direction, proportion and balance of the design without making it look too realistic.

Notice that no details like eyes, nose and mouth distract your gaze from the overall unity of the design.

76
Attic hydria, or water pot, 21.9 in. (55.5 cm.) high, painted by the 'Antimenes Painter' around 525 BC. (Reproduced by kind permission of the Victoria and Albert Museum, London.)

The scenes on the sides of the hydria are quite fascinating, both from a pictorial point of view and from that of a designer. This example, with no perspective as we know it, is full of wonderful shapes and patterns, many of which could be isolated and used out of context; the chariot wheel and horses' legs; the curve of the horses' manes, tails and reins; even the pattern of shapes on the top border round the shoulder of the hydria are full of design ideas.

52

The more stylized figures of men, women and horses on Greek vases are full of detail, and are particularly interesting because some of them have black backgrounds with orange and white figures, giving a negative appearance which is most unusual. A design using ideas from Greek vases worked in pulled thread embroidery on a very dark fabric would certainly be very exciting and effective.

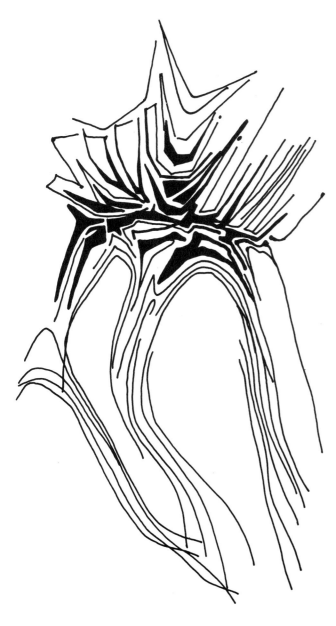

77

A free-flowing section of drapery on a figure from the Parthenon, about 400 BC. The folds appear to square off in some parts, giving a very different type of line from some other reliefs which show drapery of a swirling nature. The type of design drawn here can be expressed in many techniques, including those which make use of gathered, pleated, smocked and 'scrunched' fabric.

78

This drawing, also from a carved Greek figure, could be developed in various ways for use with methods like knitting and crochet, or with a less textural technique such as appliqué.

The 'window method' of capturing only part of the design would be useful here if a smaller section is required, but if you feel like tackling a complicated project try super-imposing the drapery shown in Fig. 37 to make a mixture of black, grey and white lines. To eliminate lines from the one underneath, take several small pieces of white paper and slide them around between the two drawings, thus blotting out the parts not required.

The Ages of Stone, Bronze and Iron

Many local museums have large collections of implements and weapons made in the thousands of years before civilization as we know it. Often these objects are crude, and few are particularly decorative, but some do possess very interesting shapes, colours and textures which, if studied in a new light, can inspire embroidery designers.

Museums frequently have displays of varioussized tools and weapons, made of chipped and flaked flint and bone belonging to the Old Stone Age (Paleolithic period), which ended in Europe about ten thousand years ago. Note the colour of the stones, the arrangement of light and shade, and those lines which are important to the whole shape and the textures. Parts of them may shine where pieces have been chipped away, while other parts may be rough. When sketching at the museum, it helps to indicate these parts on your drawing with lines, dots or even a few brief notes.

New Stone Age (Neolithic period, about 10,000-5,000 BC) implements show a little more sophistication and polish than earlier ones, and smoothness and shine are often more apparent; the shapes

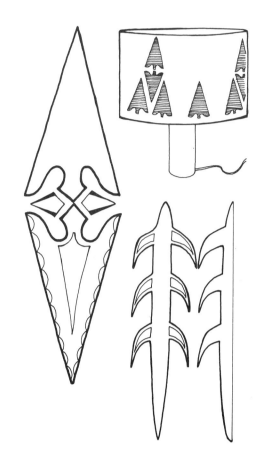

79
This drawing is of a large neolithic hand axe found near Reading, England, and now in the museum there.

It would have been both time-consuming and unnecessary to have drawn all the lines dividing the facets, so I noted instead the shapes of the facets themselves as they were caught by the light from one side, and the shaded ones on the other side. The ridge down the centre could perhaps be treated in a bolder way than the rest of the design. Note that a large area has been left plain, making the treatment on the other parts much more effective in contrast.

80
A small, daintily-shaped spear-head is a tiny motif with many possible applications; a lampshade of pulled thread work or shadow work, a border design for table linen, or a cushion using four motifs to form a square.

The little bone fishing hook is another such motif; note particularly the background shape formed when two are placed together.

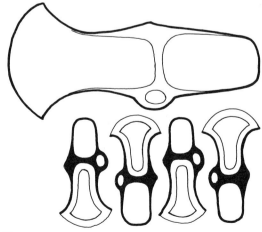

81
A palstave, or axe-head, made of bronze is a very pleasing shape. Like the spear-head and fishing hook, it has useful applications as a small repeat motif.

become more intricate, and pottery is included, for about this time men began to live in village communities and to store their food in pots made of dried but unfired clay.

In the Bronze Age (in Britain, about 1,400-600 BC), objects and weapons were fashioned in a more ornamental style. Axes, daggers, swords and knives were often buried with skeletons or the ashes of the dead, and show a satisfying smoothness and cleanness of shape. Brooches, or fibulae, of bronze can be seen in most museums.

The Iron Age, (in Britain, about 1,000-500 BC, overlapping with the Bronze Age) produced tools and weapons made of a much harder metal. However this changeover from bronze to iron was very gradual, and for a long time objects of both metals, as well as stone, flint and bone, continued to be made. Early Iron Age craftsman also learned how to enamel their shields and jewelry. Look for the lovely designs of chevrons, lozenges and concentric circles, and the extravagant curves on the backs of iron and bronze mirrors.

The Celts

The Celts were a widely spread pagan people, mentioned by Greek writers as early as the sixth century BC. They occupied most of the countries of Europe in their various stages of culture until the Romans gradually took over their lands, including England. Strongholds of Celtic resistance remained in such inaccessible places as Scotland, Wales, Ireland, the Isle of Man and the lesser populated districts of Cornwall and Brittany, where the Celtic language continued to be spoken for some time afterwards.

To comment significantly on Celtic art would take far too long; it is enough to say that styles vary with their tribal connections — a fascinating subject for research. Large quantities of Celtic objects have been found in graves, the most treasured finds being bronze mirrors, shields and jewelry, of which they were passionately fond. Their craftsmen were skilled in the use of bronze, iron, gold, silver and alloys, and decorated their work with symbols, fantastic animals, spirals and swirling and geometric designs.

The Belgic people — Celts who came from northeast Gaul to settle in south-east England — made many contributions to British art in the form of pottery and coinage, and also in the art of toolmaking. They may have invented the plough. Another Celtic design will be found in the section on Ground Marks.

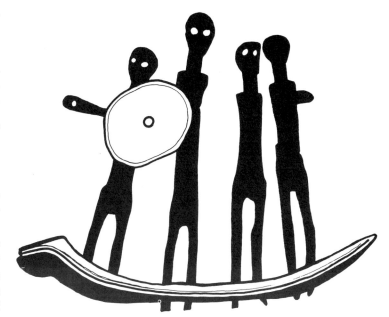

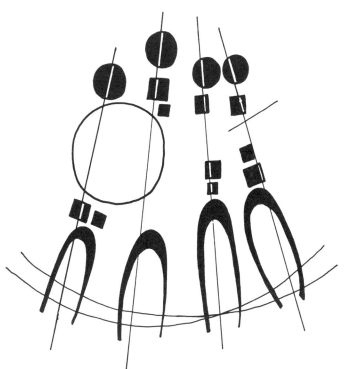

82a and b
This Bronze Age pinewood toy boat was found in Yorkshire, England. I present it here in silhouette form to emphasize the interesting arrangement of the shapes rather than the shapes themselves.

In 82b I have indicated in an even more basic manner the arrangement that appealed to me, by a series of lines, squares and circles of which the original seemed to be composed. Much more could be done, in embroidery, to make this into a completely abstract design — perhaps by the use of machine 'scribble-stitchery' on the background, while still maintaining the upward direction of each motif.

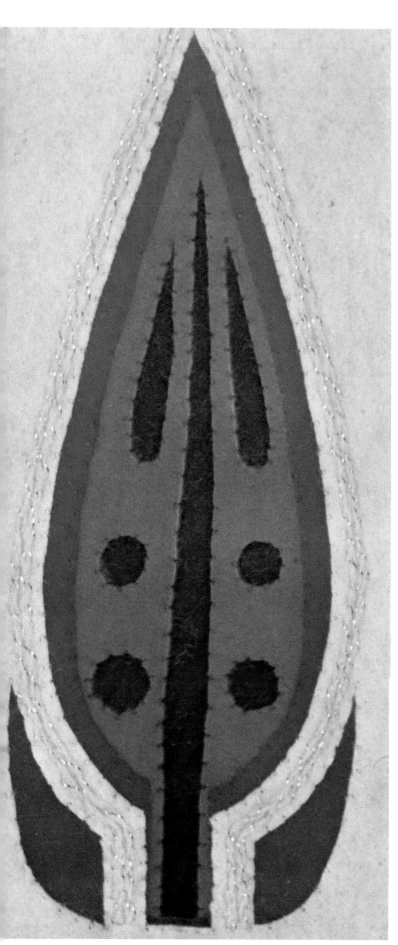

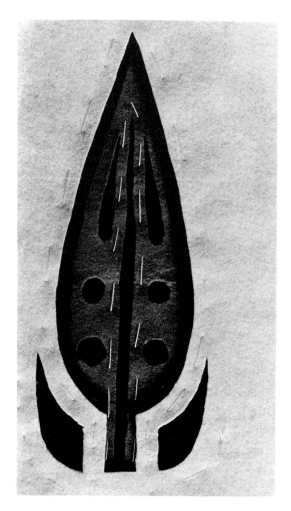

83a and b

This is a design taken from a Bronze Age spear-head of around 900 BC. It is worked in reverse appliqué and measures 6.7 x 2.5 in. (15 x 6.5 cm.).

The first stage, before stitching, is illustrated: the fabric is cut to reveal the layers underneath, and then tacked down. As the fabric is felt, the edges needed no turning under. The finished piece has been sewn down on all edges with tiny, evenly spaced stitches in matching sewing cotton, the only decoration being two lines of white lurex and wool mixture couched round the edge of the main shape. The two wing-shapes at the base are my own additions to help the balance of the design.

84

Opposite

Four Egg Cosies based on a stirrup iron of the Anglo-Saxon period in England (see **88** and **89**). You will see that very little of the stirrup-iron shape has been changed for use on these little egg cosies. The squared strap-hole on the top has been fully incorporated into the design using a related colour which has been repeated in the fly stitch below. Each one measures 5¾ in. high and 3½ in. (14.6 x 9 cm.) wide. They were made by the author.

The close affinity between the art of the Celts in Britain and that of the Scandinavian Vikings is hardly surprising when we remember that Christianity was introduced into Norway and Sweden by Irish missionaries. As a result of a well-established style of ornamentation shown in the carvings of intertwining scrollwork and animals, and a more recent leaning towards the use of Christian symbols, we find an interesting mixture of the two. Sometimes the bodies of dogs, birds, snakes and fantastic animals tangle with branches decorating a carved cross or a manuscript, and sometimes such a decoration is used on the outside of a church.

86
This design on a seventh century BC bronze vessel from Sopron in Hungary is most 'embroiderable'. The little people spinning, weaving and playing the harp, have nothing more than triangles for bodies, these shapes being repeated on the lower parts of the design.

85
Decoration on the stave church at Urnes in Norway, about AD 1050. It represents the world tree which, in Scandinavian tradition, is the gigantic evergreen ash tree supporting the universe.

The idea of the tracery and intertwining arms of the branches may suggest the use of metal threads to form a linear design, or surface stitches in related colours, lines of closely packed machine stitches, corded quilting or tubes of fabric. A decorative animal of your own invention could be included in the same manner as the one shown here.

87a and b
I have partly rendered this Celtic human head motif in a style which would be suitable for any of the counted thread methods. It would also adapt well to other techniques, as the various areas of the design are well defined and need only be simplified.

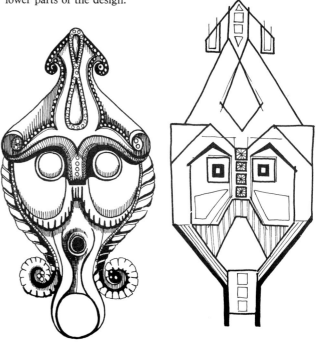

58

The Anglo-Saxons

Before the end of the Roman occupation in England about AD 410, the Saxons came from Holland, Denmark and Northern Germany. Many readers will know of the famous Anglo-Saxon poem about Beowulf of Gotland, which gives us valuable information about these people and their lives.

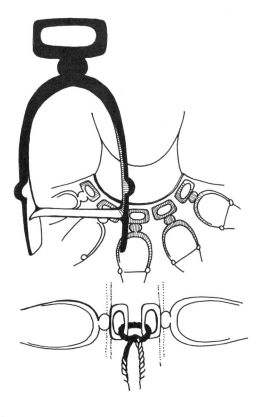

88
An Anglo-Saxon stirrup iron makes an attractive shape which could be used to decorate a neckline, or the hem and the sleeve edges of a dress, or down the front as in the arrangement shown in the lower drawing. The two ring shapes could be the site of holes through which a lace could be passed for fastening. Unusual fastenings of this kind are visually much more interesting than hooks and eyes, zips and press studs, however efficient these modern closures may be.

89
Anglo-Saxon stirrup iron (see **84**).

90
From the Sutton Hoo Treasure is this design of boars from a shoulder clasp worn by the chieftain whose possessions were buried there along with his ship. The boar played a significant part in the mythology of the pagan Celts because of his attributes of bravery, strength and virility.

59

91 and 92

Layout of Red fabrics and threads with detail of Head based on Isle of Lewis Chessmen.

Here can be seen a selection of materials one might collect together before starting to design. The black, white and grey background seemed to be a good starting point for an embroidery based on the chessmen using various reds, pinks and silvers for the figures. Gathering together all available materials of the desired colour-scheme in this way will often suggest design and technique ideas more readily than pencil and paper.

Areas of finer embroidery may be worked separately on a hoop and then applied to the background in the appropriate place. The king's face was a composite design made up of parts of several kings' faces, embroidered by the author on a hoop 4 in. diameter (10 cm.). The crown, hair and beard are needleweaving, with tiny silver and red beads and couched silver threads here and there. The eyes are spiders' webs, buttonhole and fly stitches, with satin stitches on the cheeks, mouth and moustache to give a contrastingly smooth appearance. (Refer to key overleaf).

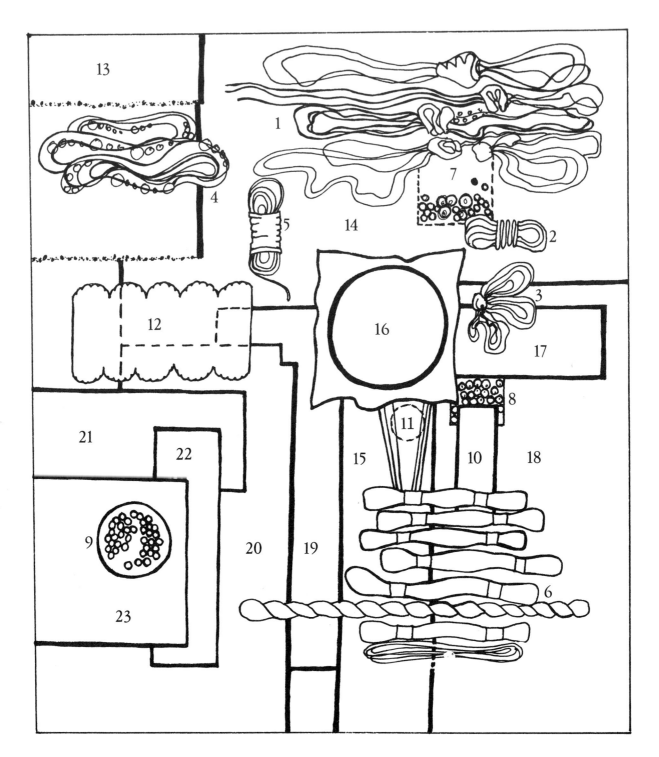

93

The Anglo-Saxons.
Key Notes for photograph based on
Isle of Lewis Chessmen.
 1. Textured wools
 2. Crochet cotton
 3. Chenille
 4. Textured wool
 5. Fine plastic tube
 6. Stranded cotton and silk
 7. Fine silver beads and sequins
 8. Silvered wooden beads
 9. Small coloured beads
10. Silver plastic 'leather'

11. Plastic net vegetable bag
12. Silver lace edging
13. Nylon net
14. Woollen furnishing fabric
15. Dupion
16. Embroidered detail of Chessman's head
17. Rayon lining material
18. Felt
19. Cotton poplin
20. Evenweave wool
21. P.V.C.
22. Velvet
23. Leather

They were skilled calligraphers, artists, weavers and metalworkers, as can be seen from the many artifacts which have survived. These include the wonderful illustrated manuscripts of the gospels made by monks, the threads of gold found in graves and originally woven into women's head-dresses, and the vast stores of jewelry of all kinds, particularly those in the famous burial ship found at Sutton Hoo, England.

Much of their workmanship can be seen in the museums of Britain; brooches, belts, buckles, armlets and rings, pins and horse-trappings. Many designs are intricate, but can be simplified for use in embroidery design. Further Anglo-Saxon designs will be found in the section on Jewelry, and in Chapter 8, *Some ways of making a design*.

94
Some of the twelfth-century walrus ivory chessmen from Uig on the Isle of Lewis, Outer Hebrides, Scotland.

95
The carving on this tree was done over one hundred years ago by Australian aborigines living on the edge of the Bogan River at Nevertire. It now stands on the property of Geoff Hunt. The carving is only 9 in. (23 cm.) wide because the tree has grown over it, giving a rolled effect down the edges. The tree stands 4 ft 6 in. high (137.25 cm.) and no one explanation for its use has been found either by present-day aborigines or other residents who know of similar carved trees in the area bearing the same design of irregular diamonds.

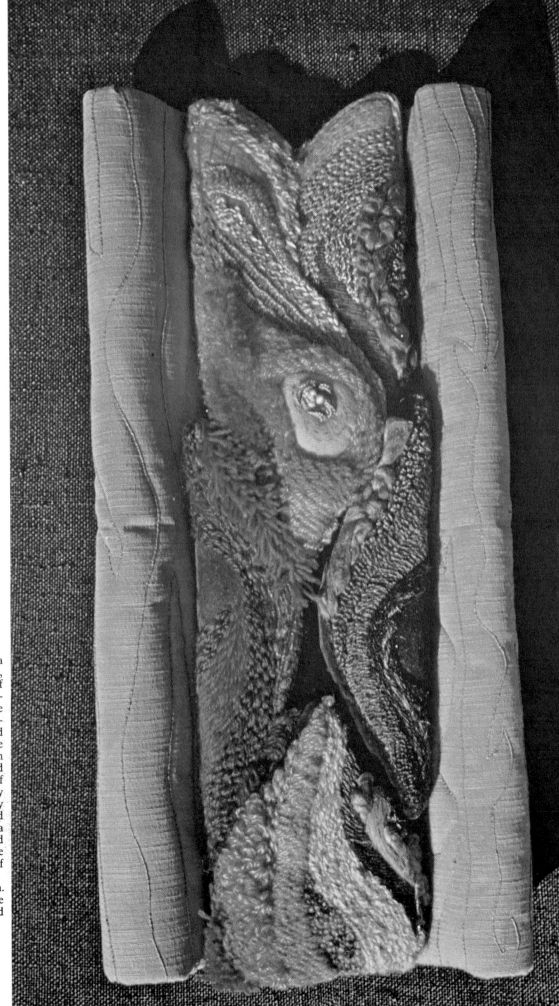

96

Cheryl Sly, a textile diploma student at Wagga Wagga, Australia, created this high relief panel on shaped pieces of single-thread canvas, which were embroidered to form three-dimensional shapes and pulled over pieces of polystyrene of the required depth. They were then attached to the velvet-covered base, giving an impression of deeply carved areas, roughly textured wood grain and knotty bumps. The side rolls were lined with velvet, then covered with a textured furnishing fabric, and machine quilted to suggest the finer grains of the new growth of wood down the sides.

The panel measures 25 x 13 in. (64 x 33 cm.) overall. The side rolls are 3 in. (7.5 cm.) deep and wide.

12 Ethnic sources

Australian Aboriginal and Oceanic art

The aborigines of Australia have many differing styles of art depending on the area: some paint on bark, some on rock, some carve on trees and other objects, and some tribes are well known for their painted baskets made in a twining technique.

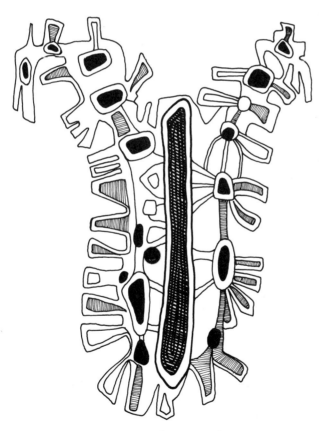

97
A design of magic healing crystals painted on the body of an Australian medicine man. This design has great potential for interpretation into embroidery, using a wide variety of methods, including metal thread embroidery, knitting with appliqué and padded shapes, cutwork, or needleweaving with tufted areas.

98
Female figure from a painting on Nourlangie Rock, Northern Territory, Australia. The composition from which this figure is taken was painted in brown and white on brown rock.

Carving, incising, fluting and pecking are some of the ways in which the aborigines decorate wooden objects such as paddles, shields, spear throwers, ceremonial boards, boomerangs and clubs. The shallow grooves are made with implements of stone, bone and teeth; they are closely packed together and often filled with red and white pigment.

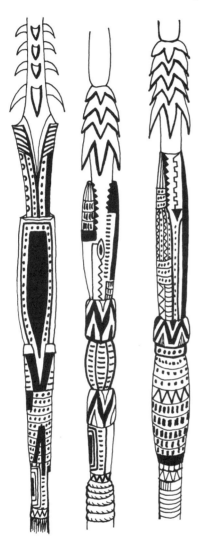

99 and 100
New Guinea is a rich source of design, especially those areas around the Sepik River valley where many carved and painted objects, mainly with abstract designs, are found. Those on the houseboards shown here were made by the Telefolmin and Faiwolmin people, who live in the Sepik River valley near the border with Papua.

These bold designs would, I feel, look well on rugs either for use on the floor or hanging on the wall. The clear lines and well defined areas of pattern would adapt well for shaggy pile or hooked rugs. They could also be used to decorate a knitted garment, perhaps as a lower border, a central panel or a single motif, on mittens or on a scarf. Use graph paper to work out the pattern, using one square to one stitch.

101
This spiral pattern is taken from the tattooed face of a Maori warrior or chief. The spiral is one of the characteristic elements in Maori art, and is found on many wooden objects as well as on the human body.

To make the design simpler, and to eliminate the symmetry, place a cover over one half down the centre line, and see the remaining swirling lines as stitchery—perhaps goldwork.

67

Although the many islands that comprise Oceania each have their individual styles of art, these are nevertheless closely related to each other because of the geographical similarity between the islands and many thousands of years of influence by people from other countries, particularly China and South America. Though bearing designs typical of a particular region, similar artifacts are found all over Oceania; they include statues, masks of ancestors (except in Polynesia), ornamental pieces, canoes, paddles, grave posts, houseboards and other objects of daily use, some of which have a hidden symbolic meaning.

Africa

African art is, unfortunately, too often thought of as comprising only carvings and masks. Though these may well represent the art of the African negro, there is much more than this for us to draw upon for design ideas. From the gaily coloured rugs, carpets and garments of Moroccan bazaars to the leatherwork, silverwork and weaving of the Sahara tribesmen whose brilliant camel blankets contrast so well against the buff of camels and sand—all these impressions can inspire embroiderers if they are used to create not copies but exciting, stimulating, individual designs.

102, 103, 104
Three-dimensional head based on an Ibibio mask of Southern Nigeria. This free-hanging head is an example of how crochet and rug-hooking can be used with great success alongside embroidery of a more conventional nature, in this case, quilting.

The foundation used for the head, though not the hat, was rug-canvas. The face was made of two layers of padded and quilted felt, worked flat; the nose and eyelashes were made separately and sewn on to the bottom layers. Unspun nylon, courtelle and terylene were used for the hair; this was easily pulled into tufts and latchet-hooked through the canvas. Here and there long crocheted chains were threaded through the foundation and left to hang freely.

After the head had been sewn up the back, the conical hat of rug-wool was crocheted on, being worked round and round in alternate rows of double-crochet and half treble, decreasing all the way up. A covered wooden ring was added for hanging, then crocheted bobbles of silver and white wool were attached round the edge of the hat to add to the three dimensional effect and the peak at the base of the hat was finished off with a large, crochet-covered tassel of the same rug-wool.

To keep the shape of the head, hoops of strong covered wire were stitched to the inside before closing up the base of the head with a disc of white felt. The head, made by the author, measures 23 in (58.4 cm.) from the top of the hat to the chin.

Masks seem to be an essential part of the art of primitive countries today, and of most ancient civilizations too. They do, of course, play an indisputably important role in the structure and religious life of primitive societies, for they are worn to change the identity of the wearer into a spirit, demon or animal, and as such often have exaggerated and grotesque features, leaving onlookers in no doubt as to their disposition and authority.

105
Ibibio mask of Southern Nigeria (Museum of Ethnography).

69

Masks are still used today in the classical theatre of China, and in other eastern countries for religious and ceremonial purposes. In Britain they are still worn by Morris dancers. Americans wear caricatures of the seven dwarfs and Mickey Mouse at carnivals, and American Indians donned the masks and hides of buffaloes to lull the herds into a false sense of security. Almost every country of the world has its masks, ancient or modern; they are a tangible means of expressing our fantasies.

Children, who have few inhibitions about such things, love to wear masks, and they are fun to make. For the embroiderer, they offer design ideas to be executed in any medium, for the very controlled type of design or for the wildest and most exuberant.

Here we have an opportunity to make use of a wide assortment of 'found' objects, certain in the knowledge that they will be in keeping with the subject. Those objects frequently attached to masks include shells, bells, feathers, rings, all kinds of disc shapes and beads, plaited, knitted and wrapped fibres such as wool, hair, raffia and leather. Macramé comes into its own here, as masks interpret well into three-dimensional and free-hanging shapes. Cardboard cylinders are useful as supports for totem-pole-like arrangements of faces.

106
Probably the best known of all African works of art are the cast bronze heads of Benin in Nigeria, the earliest of which date at least to the fifteenth century. There is great variation in the decoration of the head-dresses.

Taken section by section, an object like this may provide ideas for textural treatments in embroidery, especially of raised areas like the criss-cross of the crown, the stiffened projection, the tubular hanging side-pieces and the coils around the neck. Try to imagine these in fabrics and threads, and in colours.

107
The seventeenth-century kingdom of Ashanti occupied the region which is now Ghana. Its rich gold deposits made the inhabitants so wealthy that gold dust was their currency, weighed against little brass weights of beautiful workmanship, now collected by museums. Some of these are shown here, with little brass boxes in which the gold dust was carried. The subjects used as designs for the weights include fish, insects, animals, human beings, plants, spear-heads and other miscellaneous objects. Simple little motifs like these have many uses for embroiderers; they can be used in conjunction with larger designs, for small objects. Some of them may suggest cutwork, appliqué or goldwork.

108

The pronounced hippopotamus-like features of this otobo mask used by the Ekine society of the Kalabari of the Niger delta represent a water spirit which is partly human. This seems to me to be the kind of motif which would look most effective in brilliant fabrics and bold stitches, or brightly-coloured felts on a highly patterned background. It would also adapt very well to canvas embroidery and patchwork.

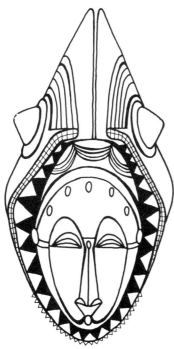

109

This African mask is from the Baulé; it is made of hard wood, stained brown and polished. Basically a very simple shape, it is full of other interesting smaller shapes which could help the development of an embroidery in high relief with the hat part gradually coming well away from the background, then receding deeply in to the edge of the face. The face shape could be padded firmly or perhaps worked in reverse appliqué.

It would also be possible, with a little ingenuity, to make this an entirely three-dimensional, free-hanging piece, with some form of decoration (perhaps another face) on the other side.

The American Indians

American Indian designs have always been popular among designers of woven fabrics because of their adaptability to the directions of warp and weft, but comparatively few of these designs have as yet been used as inspiration by embroiderers. Though it is true that many of these designs are geometrical, symmetrical and highly stylized (some to the point of abstraction), in many methods of embroidery this type of design is desirable—*not* simply a copy in cross-stitch, but worked in a way which will introduce an original touch to what might other-wise be just another pattern. What makes these designs unique and instantly recognizable is the bold way in which they use controlled but

110

One of the best-known products of the semi-nomadic Navaho tribe are the famous blankets. The Navahos occupy a reservation in northern Arizona, north-west New Mexico and southern Utah; they are the largest tribe in North America and are highly skilled weavers and silversmiths.

As well as blankets and rugs, Navaho weavers make dresses, shirts, ponchos, saddle blankets and sashes, all of which are highly prized for their beauty and workmanship.

brilliant colour, the good proportions and use of spaces between elements of a design, and their suitability for the objects which they decorate.

There is no shortage of material from this source; the Indians of America are still producing articles of excellent quality, bearing designs full of symbolism and hidden meaning, which have been handed down to them over the centuries. Photographs in books, museums of ethnography and private collections will provide the designer with ideas for every occasion, for borders, motifs, arrangements of solid shapes, diaper patterns, free-hanging objects, weaving projects, cushion and coverlet ideas, for patchwork, appliqué—both reverse and ordinary, all forms of counted thread work and knitting; these are only a few of the many possible applications.

Designs are also to be found in basketry, on totem poles, on pottery, on the bark and skin paintings used for tents, clothes and shields, and on masks, sand paintings and silverwork.

113

This panel of rectangles was designed by Cree Indians and worked in porcupine quills. My sketch shows how different the effect can be when the areas of black and white are reversed.

111

Many blanket designs are made up of the triangle and the lozenge in such a wide variety of arrangements that one hardly ever sees a pattern repeated exactly. Use is made of black and white as in the top and centre patterns, and black, red, brown and white as in the lower one.

114

Another version of the stepped diamond pattern can be seen on this Ojibway design from a woven hemp bag. Note the different centres to the diamonds—this could be used to introduce a contrasting and vivid splash of colour into an otherwise sombre scheme of muted colours.

To repeat the row for an all-over pattern, the diamonds may be staggered in the spaces between, or arranged point to point to create larger diamond-shaped spaces where a small motif could be placed. To create a diagonal all-over pattern or one with a zig-zag direction, place more rows of the same pattern above and below so that the diamonds join top right to bottom left, and so on.

115

Opposite

Basketry reached a high standard among the Indians of California, where it became their most important art form. The coastal Pomo Indians have excelled above all others: their work possesses the greatest variety of design arrangements, the most technical skill and the widest range of sizes from the tiniest pot to man-sized ones.

Both coiling and twining methods are used with geometric patterns, often in a diagonal slant. Lozenges, diamonds and squares are also found, like this lidded pot which is partly covered by tiny glass beads, a common form of decoration among the Pomos. Feathers are sometimes interwoven on special baskets used as gifts.

A simple geometric design such as this one could be worked in any counted thread stitch, though canvas embroidery would show its colours better than a monochrome method. The fibre of the pot is purple and orange, now faded; the beads are black, white, yellow, blue and red. It is 9.5 in. (24 cm.) high.

112

This sketch of a rug shows how a simple motif can be repeated and reversed to form a compact, shape-filling design. Cut paper (newsprint) can be used to plan the shapes on a large piece of rug canvas; pin them on and then draw round them with a thick felt-tipped pen. Here again, the white spaces in between the black shapes form a design of their own. The negative and positive shapes could, on another rug, change roles to make a pair having the same design but with different colour accents.

South America

All over South America we find numerous examples of wonderful designs in ceramics, architecture, metalwork, sculpture, mosaicwork and textiles — arts which were brought to a very high standard by the various civilizations from as early as 2000 BC until the overthrow of the Incas, which began in AD 1532. The Olmecs, the Mayas, the Aztecs and the Incas had a most comprehensive and exciting range of artistic abilities, and their achievements stand comparison with any produced in other parts of the world both before and since. With this wide range of material to inspire us we should never be short of ideas for embroidery designs.

As well as the better-known Aztec and Maya, there were other civilizations, both preceding and following these, whose work in various branches of art takes completely different forms. Some designs are realistic, even humorous, some formal and stylized, and some completely abstract. Many of the motifs are repeated on pottery, textiles and architectural sculptures, and are still used in the present-day handiwork of Mexico, Bolivia and Peru.

No one has been able to say exactly when the first weavers of Peru began to produce the beautiful fabrics for which the country is famous, but recent excavations have proved that weaving was carried out as much as 2,000 years ago.

Many Peruvian textiles from ancient times were found in graves in the coastal desert region, and were preserved in excellent condition because of the dryness of the sand and the climate. Textiles found in more northerly areas of Peru, where a

116
A simplified drawing of one of the attendant figures from the great monolithic doorway at Tiahuanaco in Bolivia, which is one of the most important archaeological sites in South America. The doorway shows in perfect detail stylized representations of the human figure, the condor and the puma, figures which are also found in abstract form in textiles and ceramics.

117
The source of this design is the attendant figure motif from the monolithic doorway at Tiahuanaco. If you compare the two, you will realize that this one is actually the same basic motif, depicted in an abstract style for use on a woven shirt of the period. Parts of the figure are still recognisable, though all are now rendered into geometric shapes fitting perfectly into a rectangle.

Many embroiderers would enjoy working out a design of this kind, paying as much attention to the spaces left in the background as to all the other shapes. Many kinds of treatment are possible, used with brilliant colours against a contrastingly dark background for best effect.

damper climate prevails, have not withstood the effects of time to the same extent.

Great care was taken in the preparation of mummies for burial; they were wrapped in many layers of finest gauze weave and embroidered mantles of great size which were obviously made for this specific purpose. These are the famous Paracas mantles, covered with the most intricate and brilliant designs of geometrical and semi-naturalistic forms. In the women's graves were found plaited rush workbaskets, always containing several balls of wool and cotton, some woven and some unwoven, spindles, weaving swords and shed-sticks — everything, in fact, which the industrious woman would have need of in her next life.

The equally famous Nazca textiles, dating from the fifth century AD, were of a technically perfect woven construction, as were those of the later Tiahuanaco and Inca civilizations, though they differed from each other in design while using similar subjects. Men, gods and spirits, animals, fish, birds and geometric motifs, especially the stepped fret (or square spiral), were all treated in a highly stylized and sometimes completely abstract manner, with no natural elements of design introduced at all.

There is so much to be said about the skill of the Peruvian weavers that I can only refer interested readers to the bibliography for further information. The subject is extensive and fascinating. Meanwhile let us look at some of the better-known motifs and try to catch the spirit of them in our own work.

118
The American Indian often decorated his horse as lavishly as himself, and this detail of a horse's trappings shows the great care taken to achieve a splendid effect.

The part shown here is the crupper, the top end of which was fastened to the saddle cloth (or saddle for those who used one); the padded loop passed under the horse's tail. The decorated side panels would then lie along the back of the horse, with the elaborate leather fringe hanging down on either side. The central panel design is made of dyed porcupine quills, a type of decoration widely practised until glass beads were introduced by Europeans, when beadwork started to take the place of quillwork. The two circular motifs are probably painted on to the leather. The fringing is wrapped part way down to add to the design, and pieces of bone or teeth are still attached to some of the ends.

Hanging in this position it may give the designer ideas for a project, woven or embroidered, knitted or crocheted, wrapped or knotted.

119
This figure from the Chimu dynasty (Peru, around AD 1400) forms the handle of a gold ceremonial knife inlaid with turquoise. It would be quite simple to adapt this square little man to a series of geometric shapes for embroidery; there are many ways of using a compact motif such as this, and certainly as many methods of embroidering it.

120
Above
An adaption of a similar motif from Tiahuanaco has been used here on this enamelled silver bracelet from Peru, together with the figure which occupies the central position on the monolithic doorway, and the feline motif. The central figure is probably an important god holding staves which are thought to represent a spear-thrower and a quiver of darts.

121
The owner of the bracelet in the preceding illustration, Sheila Paine, also made and embroidered this full-length skirt of white cotton. The design is appliquéd, using the same bright colours as on the bracelet, with herringbone and couching stitches to outline each motif.

This is an excellent example of the way in which a design of primitive or ancient origin can be adapted for embroidery on dress; it could also have been knitted or woven, as similar motifs are by present-day South American Indians.

122
Right
This detail of the central figure shows the treatment used: bold and colourful so that the full effect of the shapes is not lost with the movement of the skirt.

13 Signs, symbols and objects

Calligraphy, symbols and knotwork

Embroiderers use ancient letter forms with great success in a wide variety of methods; many of them can be used in counted thread embroidery because of their geometric nature. Some are curvilinear and can be used to fulfil almost any design purpose, as repeating patterns, borders, or single motifs, or as larger, more complex designs for panels and hangings.

Before man ever created a true representation of those things most familiar to him, he drew symbols. He gave the sun and moon, men and women,

123
The shapes made by the spaces between letters can be just as interesting as the letters themselves, as can be seen in this design which is based on runic characters. The characters in the design shown here are used upside-down as well as the right way up; the background shapes have been divided up also, so that neither it nor the characters are dominant.

124
The Sumerians, who at first used pictographic writing, later developed a much quicker and more useful method of recording events called cuneiform, meaning 'wedge-shaped'. This consisted of wedge-shaped impressions made by a stylus on damp clay, similar to these marks seen here.

This design, inspired by cuneiform writing, consisted at first of only half the arrangement, which was then turned upside-down and placed over the other half slightly lower down.

125
The raised characters from which this design was made were carved in limestone in south west Arabia in the first century, AD. The original carving can be seen in the British Museum.

They have been used both ways up and in any order.

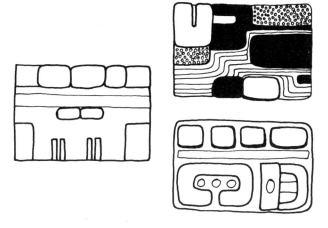

126
The ancient Maya of Central America developed a form of writing which consisted of pictures, or pictographs. The neat little characters are beautifully contained within rounded rectangles and ovals, and would make excellent designs for corded and padded quilting, and for rugs.

128
Kufic lettering is one of the oldest and most ornamental of all types of cursive script. From early Islam, it was named after the city of Kufa and was often integrated with the decorative brickwork for which many mosques and public buildings are famous.

The inscription shown here was carved into the stonework at the entrance of Pir i Baqran Sanctuary at Linjan, a small village south of Isfahan in Iran. AD 1299-1311.

127
The three circular shapes are Stone-Age cave drawings found in Lovo in the Congo region of Africa. The two swastika symbols were found on oriental carpets, and would make attractive arrangements for patchwork cushions.

129
Many designs, including lettering on the outsides of buildings, are worked in coloured tiles and bricks; these tiled letters could be the basis of a design for counted thread work, particularly pulled or canvas work. It could easily be knitted into a garment or adapted for corded quilting.

The inscription is taken from a detail of tile work round the main door of a large architectural complex known as Char Bakr, outside the city of Bukhara in the USSR.

130
I made this cushion in canvas embroidery, using ordinary 4-ply knitting wools in a variety of stitches. All the designs are from Peruvian textiles and are arranged so that the colours achieve maximum contrast, with the darker ones slightly more dominant. The colours range through yellows, oranges and browns to white, and the cushion measures 23.7 x 16 in. (61 x 40.5 cm.).

If you look at the patterns on Peruvian fabrics, you will see that some motifs do not quite fit on at the ends of the rows, and occasionally have been adapted to fill the gaps. When I made the cushion I purposely omitted to measure patterns and threads, so that sometimes my motifs fitted the rows perfectly and sometimes not. Even my background wool ran out on one stripe and I had to continue with a different one. Stitches however, should always be correctly and evenly worked. Canvas stitches should always cover the canvas completely, especially on cushions and upholstery.

131
The fish motif was a favourite one amongst Peruvian weavers. This is a detail of the canvas-work cushion showing the stitches and the threads used; white for the body of the fish, against a mid-brown background. As in the row of llamas, the tent stitch in the background was reversed at regular intervals between motifs, and double thread was often used in order to cover the canvas completely.

132
This is one way of treating a simple motif, in this instance a sun symbol worked on the sewing machine with Sylko in straight stitch on chamois leather over padding. The outside circle was corded underneath with fine plastic tubing. This kind of treatment would look well on a garment requiring a delicate and yet firm decoration.

133
One of the very earliest of all Christian symbols is the *Chi-Rho,* consisting of the initial letters of *XPICTOC,* which is the Greek for Jesus Christ. There are many ways of varying the dimensions of this symbol; you may feel that the X would be higher up the P, or the curve of the P smaller or larger or even squared-off to suit the method of embroidery you have chosen.

animals and life in general their own symbols, varying only slightly in form in different parts of the world over the thousands of years before Man the artist came into his own. Many of these primitive symbols have proved so apt that they are still in use today; small children still draw a circle with rays extending from it to represent the sun, and in design so do many adults.

Other signs and symbols of ancient origin can be seen in the fields of botany, astrology, astronomy, chemistry, mathematics, masons' personal signs and monograms. As in calligraphy, designers can make use of their beautiful shapes either alone, or in border designs, or linked with another symbol such as the sun or the cross.

The sun was, in fact, probably the first symbol adopted by primitive and ancient Man. It has been found scratched on cave walls, on pieces of stone and wood, and drawn on skin and paper. The sun's rays and cardinal points denote life and fertility, and the sun has been the basis of ancient religions in every part of the world (see *Some ways of making a design*).

In Ancient Egypt, the sun disc, or Aten, was the visible source of all life, creation, growth and action, and this hymn in praise of the sun was composed by Akhenaten (formerly Amenhotep IV, husband of Nefertiti) who came to the throne in 1330 BC. It was found on the walls of graves and temples in Egypt.

Hymn to Aten
Lordly thou climbest the heavenly mountain of light, eternal sun, origin of life . . .

Thou hast created the world after thy liking.

Thou gavest sustenance to all living creatures
for ever.
Thou apportionest to each his span of life.

Thou art the pounding of my heart.

All that we perceive in thy light shall perish, but thou shalt live and prosper for evermore.

The swastika, or armed cross, is thought to be the oldest Aryan symbol, denoting the movement of the seasons and believed to bring well-being. It is indeed an extremely ancient sign found all over the world, originating as a diagrammatic representation of the sun's course in the heavens, symbolizing revival and prosperity. The only countries in which it never seems to have appeared are Egypt, Babylon and Assyria.

Religious symbols are surely very familiar to most of us, but though they give us information in a simple, easily recognized and understood fashion, how many of us realize that their origins may be even more ancient than we had thought? The cross is one such symbol which has its origins in the world of Stone Age Man, being one of the oldest of all symbols and signifying the yearly renewal of the earth. It is the earliest star map, fixing the four cardinal points, and in the Christian Church it represents the cross on which Our Lord died.

The *ankh* of ancient Egypt, also call the *ansated* or looped Tau cross, was the symbol of life; it was often painted on Egyptian walls, sometimes held in the hand of a king or god.

Interlaced bands are found in many styles of art all over the world, both ancient and primitive. Probably the best known to us in the western world are the Viking designs of intertwined mythical animals, and the Celtic Irish, Scottish and Manx religious stone monuments and illuminated manuscripts. Carved stones in Cornwall also abound with these figures.

The style appeared very early in Mesopotamia, and similar examples of knotwork are to be seen in the art of China, primitive Africa, and in Byzantine and Islamic ornament, though each is rendered in its own particular style. The regularity with which these knots and interlacings are executed is quite amazing; no matter how many cords are used, there are never any mistakes. It is quite possible that the artists had made use of actual ropes or cords in laying down their designs in whatever medium they chose.

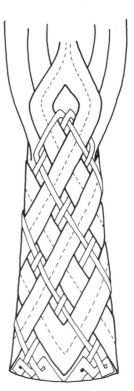

137
Even weapons, like this ornamental iron lance-point from Norway, were decorated with interlaced bands, probably of leather. It was made around AD 600-1000.

Strips of fabric, ribbon, leather, crocheted or knotted cord could also be intertwined in this way. It is, after all, merely an under-and-over weaving process.

135 and 136
The interlacing idea developed in some areas into ringwork and chain ringwork. The first technique makes use of an intertwining ring which holds together the overlapping cords, sometimes shown as a square, as here (above). Chain ringwork appears to be a continuous link of chains which connect into each other, though how this could actually be achieved without breaking each section is a mystery. This example is on a fragment of an inscribed runic cross in Bradden Church and, Isle of Man.

These ornaments could be expressed in quilting, corded and stuffed, or in real cords with sewn down covered rings. They will also hang freely, but some tend to spiral.

134
The design of a seven-branched-candlestick is taken from an oil-lamp made in Jerusalem some time in the third to fourth centuries AD. A remarkably pleasing design; this would look superb worked in metal thread.

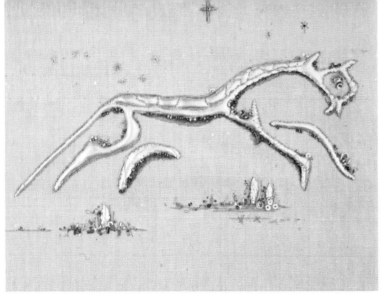

138
Panel — White Horse of Uffington.
Here the embroiderer, Georgina Anderson, has moved away
from the white-on-green colour scheme of the original
ground mark towards a delicate piece of goldwork on a
cream slub fabric. The horse has an ethereal quality about
him, created by the use of tiny beads and sequins to suggest
stars and grassy clumps. The motif is of padded gold kid,
couched in gold thread along the back and neck to create a
broken pattern, with small amounts of black net on the
lower edges to imply depth.

The complete panel measures 14 x 9¼ in. (35.5 x 23.5
cm.).

140
Another panel based on the White Horse of Uffington, also
worked by Cynthia Sparks, but this time in a different
method.

This version was worked on phosphor bronze wire, of
twenty-one threads to the inch (about nine threads to the
centimetre). Fly-screen wire could also be used for this
effect. The horse was applied in a stone-coloured vinyl
furnishing fabric over Terylene wadding, using transparent
nylon thread which was waxed to make it easier to use. It
was then freely quilted with back stitch in cream cotton.
The hard outline was broken by tent stitch in cream. The
background of 'fields' was made by overlapping triangles;
black threads were used to outline the main areas with the
threads sometimes on top of and sometimes underneath the
wire, so that they appear sometimes dark (on top) or muted
(below). Further contrast was given by fillings which varied
from velvet or astrakhan stitch through simple darning
stitches to radiating and crossing long threads, again often
behind the wire. Shading was achieved by using differing
numbers of strands of cotton. The colours used were black,
greens and golden brown.

The finished piece was mounted at the front of a 3 in.
(7.4 cm.) deep box so that it would cast a shadow on a
white card at the back. The size of the actual embroidery
inside the box frame is 15.8 x 9.6 in. (40.5 x 24.5 cm.).

139
Panel — White Horse of Uffington.
The horse in this version has been placed against a patterned
fabric which was overlaid with blue and green nets, whilst
the main motif contrasts sharply in white kid and couched
cord. Some straight stitches, knot stitches and buttonhole
fillings over rings have been used to create small areas of
pattern here and there. This panel was worked by Christine
Andrews, and measures 17¼ x 10¾ in. (43.8 x 27.3 cm.).

141
The White Horse at Uffington, Berkshire, England, a
panel in Assisi work by Cynthia Sparks; it measures 9.5 x
4.2 in. (24 x 11 cm.). This beautiful ground mark was cut
out of the chalk hillside close to an existing Iron-Age hill
fort. It is thought to have been the work of Belgic settlers
during the first century BC.

The treatment here has been kept beautifully simple, as
this is one of those 'already perfect' designs. The colours
have been kept to shades of green on white evenweave linen.

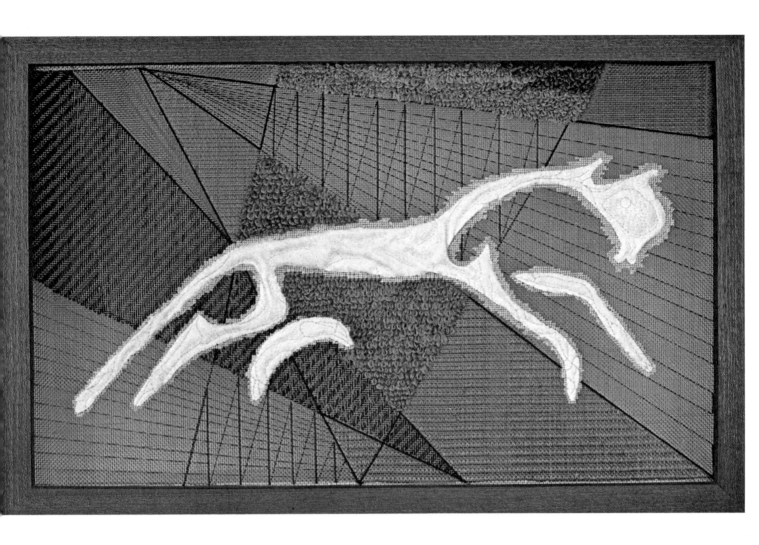

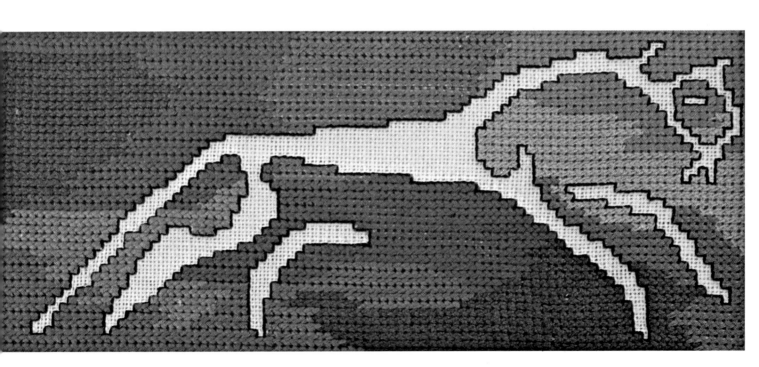

142

Knotwork can be combined successfully with other knotting techniques such as twining, braiding and macramé. The cords of this neck ornament are knotted on to a brass curtain ring, then interlaced before being knotted again. The diameter of the ring is 1.7 in. (4.5 cm), and the length of the section below the ring is 6.5 in. (17 cm.). However, there is quite a considerable length of cords with knotted ends left hanging, the centre two being the longest and measuring about 12 in. (30 cm.) from the last knot at the bottom of the photograph.

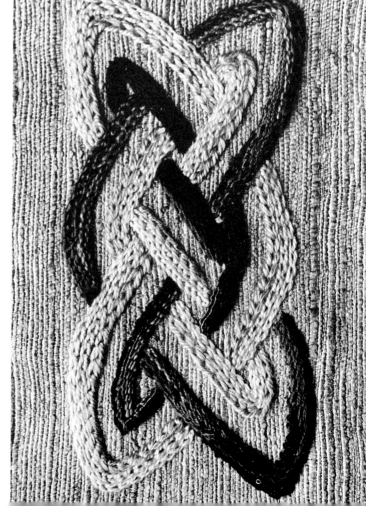

145
The White Horse of Uffington, Berkshire, England.

143 and 144 Left.

Some fascinating knotwork motifs appear to be continuous lengths of cord, like this design on a carved door from Modakeke, Ife, Africa. This type of design is found on many carvings in Africa; these two examples show how it may be adapted for embroidery.

In the quilted version, the central raised line was quilted first over very thick string by laying the string on a piece of calico on the design lines, tacking it in place, then laying green suede over the stitching close to the string. This method is an adaption of corded quilting that can be used for thick string, as it will not pull through parallel lines of stitching. This method will also allow variations in thickness in the corded method, which the other method does not. The rows on either side of the central line were quilted by the padded method, and the whole piece (suede, string and backing with stitching) was then laid over a piece of Terylene wadding and backed with another piece of calico. The design lines were worked using stab back stitch.

The stitched version shows a flatter and lighter area worked in chain stitch, shading from very pale yellow to light pinkish brown using pearl cotton and silk. The raised and darker area is worked in raised stem band in shades of brown, using pearl cotton, mattgarn and silk.

Each motif measures approximately 5.5 x 2.5 in. (14 x 7 cm.).

Ancient ground marks

Almost any book on the geography and history of a country will have an illustration of at least one type of ground mark, in the form either of a plan or of an aerial photograph. Books about the British Isles, for instance, will reveal plans of Stone Age huts, barrows (burial places), large stone circles like the ones at Avebury and Stonehenge, hill forts consisting of circular ditches and ridges, and drawings scratched on the ground which can be seen from a great distance. Of this latter type of ground mark, some of the best known are scratched on the deserts of Peru, and include a gigantic spider, a monkey, a thunderbird and other weird and monstrous creatures. These are all linear designs which would interpret very well into corded quilting. It would indeed make an interesting project to use all the ground marks of this kind from various countries in an all-over design for a quilt or some other large object.

146

Smock — White Horse of Uffington (brown and white).
Designs of this kind can also be used very successfully on
dress. This smock was made by Yvonne Povey from dark
brown cotton poplin with a border of white organza. The
horse motif was first outlined by a couched thread which
fastened the organza to the background, then stuffed from
the back with white unspun fibre, making a sharp contrast
of tones. Lines of corded quilting were introduced along the
top and bottom edges of the border to complement a nar-
rower version on the short sleeves.

The smock measures 23½ in. (59.7 cm.) from neck to
hem, and the horse motif measures 10 in. (25.4 cm.) from
nose to tail.

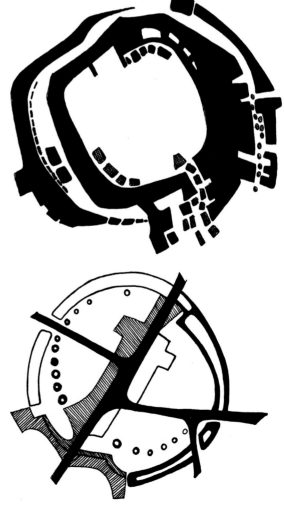

147

A Stone-Age hut at Skara Brae in the Orkney Islands,
Scotland. The shapes have been altered only very slightly,
mainly to simplify and to concentrate the smaller shapes.
Lines can be added to alleviate the solidity, but the overall
arrangement has great potential for use with a variety of
methods, such as pulled thread, blackwork, appliqué and
padding, shadow work, laid work and monochrome embroidery with surface stitches.

148

Basic design from a plan of the stone circles at Avebury,
Wiltshire, England. This could perhaps be made more
interesting by removing the geometrical shapes in the
centre and drawing more attention to the pleasing shapes
formed inside the circle by the crossing roads.

Quite often, ground plans of ancient dwellings or monuments are circular in shape, with a compactness that makes them ideal for adaptation into many forms of embroidery. Parts may be removed or added to please the designer; remember that the mark does not need to retain its identity as one particular plan. Sometimes an exciting and more complicated design can be produced by superimposing a tracing of one plan on top of another to produce different tonal effects.

Seals, stamps, coins and keys

The designs found on ancient seals are some of the most amazing and intricate to be seen anywhere. The perfection of detail found in so tiny an artifact makes them masterpieces of craftsmanship. The design was cut out of a hard material such as ivory, steatite, agate, cornelian, chalcedony, rock crystal, green jasper or glass, and was used for stamping an impression on to damp clay to mark ownership or identification. Some of the best known seals of ancient times were made in Egypt, Syria, Mesopotamia and Greece, but these were often widely distributed throughout the Ancient World for use as ornaments as well as for practical purposes.

The cylindrical seals of ancient Babylon and Phoenicia were mostly only an inch or two (2.5-5 cm.) long, often set in gold and strung on a thong to be worn round the neck or as an amulet. Large collections of seals and their impressions can be seen in the British Museum, London, and the Ashmolean Museum, Oxford.

Stamps fulfilled the same purpose as seals, and were also used to print patterns on fabrics, ceramics, confectionery and paper, both for ornamental purposes and for identification.

In the Ancient Americas they were generally made of baked clay, or occasionally stone, copper and bone. In earliest times they were made by hand, but later moulds were used. Skin, cloth and paper were stamped with vegetable and mineral dyes.

Ancient coins reveal a wealth of wonderful designs which are perfect for embroidery. Greek coins in particular are highly stylized: the designs need little simplification or rearrangement as they are so perfectly balanced within their circular boundaries. Lettering and other marks of identification can be left out, unless by their absence they detract from the unity of the design.

149
The prehistoric seal shown here is from the ancient ruined city of Mohenjo-daro in the Indus Valley. It was used about 2500 BC for stamping merchandise and other property, and as yet no-one has been able to decipher the script. Other seals of this period bear beautiful designs of oxen, elephants and rhinoceros.

150
This long design was made by a stamp found in Mexico City. The stamp was cylindrical, which accounts for the obvious repetition of the pattern after the first seven characters. The background has been changed in tone to show how the shapes between the characters can assume an equally important role. This design could be worked in several methods: because of its simplicity and boldness it would look well in appliqué—flat, padded or stuffed—quilting, canvas embroidery, surface stitchery or Assisi work.

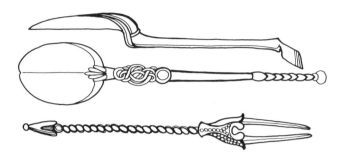

151

The head and paws of a panther, which could perhaps be worked in padded gold kid, taking the basic shape of the head as shown, and adding the other details with gold threads.

154

These spoons and fork come from countries far apart. The fork, from ancient Assyria is a beautifully decorative object which makes the perfect motif to embroider on a table mat. The spoon in the centre is an Anglo-Saxon coronation spoon. The smaller spoon on the right is made of bronze, and comes from Pompeii in Italy.

This kind of motif could also be used to decorate a table — or traycloth, either round the edges or in groups in each corner.

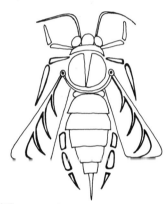

152

A rather intricate design of a bee. Stitches for this would need careful planning to express the very fine lines and tiny shapes.

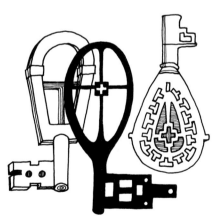

153

The three small keys shown here are of the Roman period in Britain; the one in the centre is from the Pitt Rivers Museum, Oxford, and the one on the right is a ninth-century bronze key from Canterbury, in the City Museum, Birmingham.

Such compact and interesting shapes would look well in Assisi work, monochrome and metal thread embroidery.

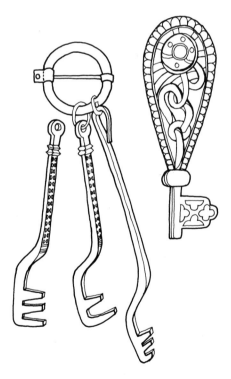

155

Though the smaller of the keys here is similar in design and age to the three Roman ones, the three on the ring are from Ullensvang in west Norway, and date from AD 400-600.

90

156
The Athenian owl, which was minted for several centuries and became the most widely used design in Ancient Greece. The richly textured surface could be expressed with beads or french knots. On a large version, the circles of the eyes could be indicated by completely oversewn curtain rings. See over. (British Museum).

The subject matter is extensive, ranging through animals, birds and fish (mythical and real), beautiful heads, fruit, plants, and objects such as lyres, buildings, shields and vases.

Most coin designs are in relief, and suggest padding and quilting if the feeling of contrast between shadow and shine is to be maintained. In many instances, corded quilting would express perfectly the fine lines of some designs, as would machine embroidery, fine beadwork and goldwork. As the designs on coins are usually compact and intricate, take care to choose a method of embroidery which will use this delicacy of feeling to best advantage.

The designs in Figs 151–2 are all from Ancient Greek coins, and could be used on embroidered pendants, buttons and brooches with great effect, as well as on table linen, small wall panels, paperweights, round box lids and greetings cards.

It seems that the older a key is, the less decoration it has, but the basic key shape is still a very interesting one for design purposes.

There are several ways of using keys in embroidery: as single motifs, for instance, or as a border for decorating bags and similar articles. Strung together on a ring they would fill a square or a circular shape perfectly. Overlap them and find the shapes in between, or use them as a border for a lampshade or in dress embroidery.

157

Owl based on **156,** embroidered by Jean Parry. Stranded cottons were mostly used, of the same colour family as the background fabric which was a heavy printed cotton. Surface stitches have been used to create a textured effect, fluffiness on the breast and ridged feathers on the wings, without striving towards realism. It measures 5¼ x 5¾ in. (13.3 x 14.6 cm).

158

Blue bag based on **159**

The girdlehanger design was appliqued in striped cotton on the sewing machine; a straight stitch *or* zig-zag will do. Herringbone stitch, knotted cable stitch and buttonhole rings were added in wool and stranded cotton. The bag was made by the author from one piece of fabric joined at the base, and measures 17 in. (43.2 cm.) from top to bottom. It has a small pocket on the reverse side and is lined with cream curtain lining.

Ceramics, glass and jewelry

Because of the diversity of styles to be found in ceramics from various parts of the world, designers have an almost unlimited supply of ideas from which to draw inspiration. Particularly good design ideas are found on Ancient Greek vessels with their intricate representations of humans and animals; these designs also have an advantage in that they are usually painted in only one main colour and are entirely two-dimensional. Geometric and stylized designs from the pottery of some American Indian tribes are excellent sources of inspiration. Looking at the pottery patterns of the Pueblos, we can find ideas for individual motifs, repeating patterns, borders, patchwork and appliqué, in fact ideas for almost any purpose and method. Geometric designs are a favourite decoration amongst primitive potters, but as well as the usual domestic pots made strictly for practical purposes we also find ceramics like those made by the ancient Peruvians in the shape of little human figures, animals, and sometimes buildings covered with bold patterns in brilliant colours. Indeed there are many sources of these pottery ornaments from the ancient world which are highly decorative, and ideal for the embroiderer to adapt. Do remember, however, that because most ceramics are three-dimensional, quite a lot of adapting and re-drawing will be necessary when rendering a pottery form into a two-dimensional design for the type of embroidery to be worked.

159
A pair of bronze girdle-hangers from Soham in Cambridgeshire, England. They date from the Anglo-Saxon period, measure 5¾ in. (14.6 cm.) in length, and were hung from the belt, or girdle, of the lady of the house more as a token of authority than for any practical purpose.

160
These designs worked in canvas embroidery are from three flat stamps of Ancient Mexico. They represent rattles which were used on ceremonial occasions. The one in the centre is worked in tent stitch going in both directions, so that the triangles at the top remain smooth and are not stepped on one side. Double knitting wool and a little stranded cotton were used on single canvas; the motifs measure between 4.4 and 4.7 in. (11 and 12 cm.) long.

161

This is a little pottery figure from Recuay, Peru, of an Inca nobleman and his llama. I felt that he was interesting enough to form an embroidery design on three levels, first the shield, then the figure, and then the llama behind.

162

The design of the Inca nobleman was worked from the bottom layer upwards, that is with the llama first. Then the figure was worked: feet and face first, the body and hat pieces next, then the knitted saddle blanket, and lastly the earplugs and shield.

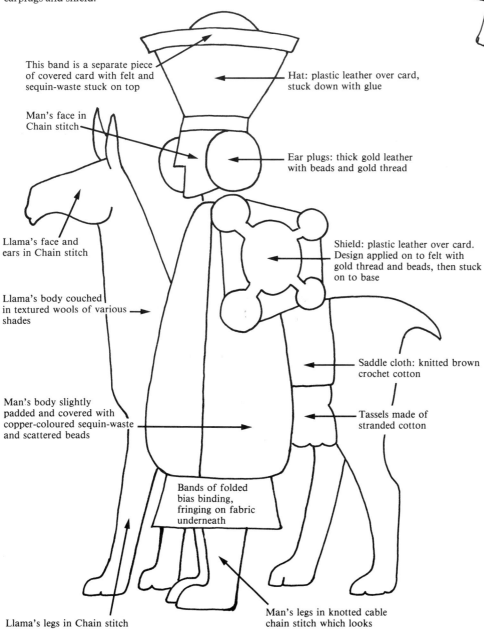

This band is a separate piece of covered card with felt and sequin-waste stuck on top

Hat: plastic leather over card, stuck down with glue

Man's face in Chain stitch

Ear plugs: thick gold leather with beads and gold thread

Llama's face and ears in Chain stitch

Shield: plastic leather over card. Design applied on to felt with gold thread and beads, then stuck on to base

Llama's body couched in textured wools of various shades

Saddle cloth: knitted brown crochet cotton

Man's body slightly padded and covered with copper-coloured sequin-waste and scattered beads

Tassels made of stranded cotton

Bands of folded bias binding, fringing on fabric underneath

Llama's legs in Chain stitch

Man's legs in knotted cable chain stitch which looks rather like knitting

163
The complete Inca nobleman panel measures 9.5 x 13.2 in.
(24 x 33.5 cm.), and is worked on golden fawn Dupion.
The padded figure is of the same material in orange, with
the llama worked in golden browns, yellows and cream.
The palest areas are also cream.

164
This detail shows the Inca nobleman's shield, which was
first cut out of card and then covered with beige plastic
leather, the edges of which were stuck on to the underside.
The embroidered motif was worked on a larger piece of
orange felt, then cut out and applied with glue; the central
part is slightly padded.

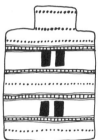
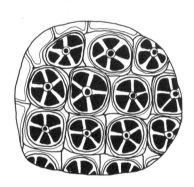

165

These little Minoan houses made of earthenware are from Knossos in Crete. The tallest of them is only about 2in. (5cm.) high. Try working them in any counted thread method, appliqué (with or without padding) patchwork, goldwork or a mixture of various other methods. They can be arranged in a variety of ways to suit different purposes.

166

This swan design from a Mycenaean vase must be familiar to many readers. It shows a range of textural effects which may suggest many ideas for treatment to the embroiderer. The birds are portrayed as pure design, and their feathers are only suggested here and there in different ways. If you look at it with half-closed eyes, you will see the swirls of movement running like a winding river from one side to the other. When you make your adaptation, try to preserve this line, as it holds the design together.

167

Millefiore glass is made by fusing together and drawing out, in a pattern, glass rods of various colours, and then slicing the rods across so that the pattern is seen in cross-section. Seaside rock is made in exactly the same way. Pieces of this glass may have been broken off the curved part of a vase or dish, giving a most unusual effect where the rods of glass have been partly exposed. This may suggest to embroiderers long tubes of fabric, crochet or knitting, laid alongside each other following a curvilinear design.

The drawing of a cross-section, or surface, of a piece of millefiore glass looks in black and white remarkably like cutwork or needleweaving. It might be an interesting idea to use small covered curtain rings for the outside ring shapes, working needleweaving across them and then attaching them to each other to form a network. With some solid shapes as contrast, this could have applications for both small- and large-scale pieces of work.

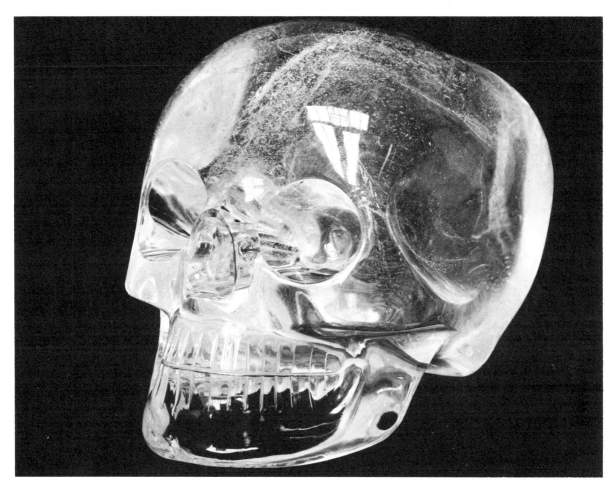

168
This is a fifteenth century rock crystal skull believed to be of Aztec origin. An amazing piece of primitive craftsmanship, this skull is full of reflections almost impossible to portray on paper. Nevertheless small areas of perfect design can be found in its shapes of shine and shadow. The original carving is in the Museum of Ethnography, London; if possible, visit the museum, walk round the skull, and study its reflections and the depth of its lights and shades. Use the 'window' method on a photograph of the skull; this will help you form an abstract design without too many other distractions.

Motifs and patterns from painted pots can be reorganized and simplified if necessary. Again, it helps to have in mind the method of embroidery, as this dictates the areas, lines and forms to be included or left out. It is sometimes helpful, too, to place a mirror on its edge on designs of this kind to double the image or to make it fit a different shape.

The art of making glass dates back very many thousands of years; small quantities of glass found in North Africa may have come from the Neolithic period. Glass beads, which were highly prized and often as expensive as natural jewels, have been found not only in Egypt, dating from around 3000 BC, but also in prehistoric graves in Assyria

and Phoenicia, Northern Europe and the Far East. The Ancient Egyptians also used glass in the manufacture of cloisonné jewelry, as can be seen from the colourful pendants and collars which we know so well, and for making small bottles and jars decorated with 'combed' chevron patterns.

Many excellent ideas for embroidery can be obtained from ancient jewelry and the various adornments of primitive people. With the inclination in recent years towards more freedom in dress and personal ornament, the styles and materials used for jewelry in ancient times are not now out-of-place. Long day clothes, flowing garments and casual evening wear are good foils for embroidered designs suggesting ancient and primitive jewelry; the embroiderer can find very many original ways of using such an abundance of material, in macramé and in fashion accessories.

Jewelry is also illustrated in other sections of this book, for it is a universal subject which has its origins in the times when Man used the only materials available to him—the same ones which are still being used today in countries both primitive and civilized.

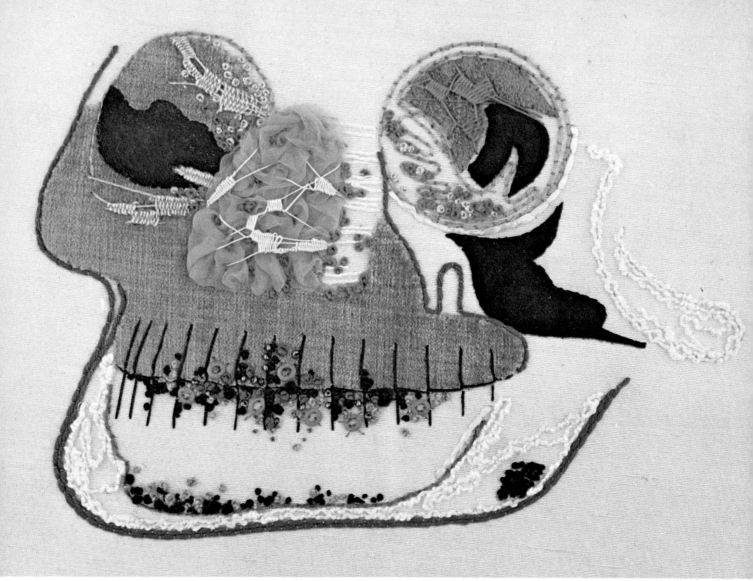

169

Brown on cream Skull embroidery. This design by Yvonne
Povey was inspired by the rock crystal Aztec skull, and
cleverly portrays the complicated reflections and shadows
to be seen within. The embroiderer made use of small
pieces of deep yellow furnishing velvet with padded suede,
finely ruched nylon, needleweaving, tiny french knots,
circular beads and couched silk and cotton. It measures
6¼ x 8¼ in. (15.9 x 21cm.).

170

Cream purse with metal clasp and chain based on **175**.
Although each separate element of the brooch has been
retained in the design it has been rearranged with the
others to fit a long, rectangular shape. The cross shapes
inside the circles are now off-centre and are defined by
gold beads with rough and smooth purl. Stuffed quilting
was used to accentuate the rest of the circles, and the fine
outlining was worked in split stitch of the same colour
as the Dupion background. The purse was embroidered
and sewn onto a purchased frame by the author, and
measures 9 x 5½ in. (22.9 x 14cm.).

171

The shapes of vases, bottles and jars are often interesting enough to use as the basis of a design such as this. You should also be aware of the spaces created between the shapes, as these are very important to the whole design. Lines are used to keep the shapes together, to relate them to each other, and to create other interesting shapes in between. No texture has been indicated here, but it would make a much more varied design which would be livened up considerably if smooth and rough surfaces juxtaposed.

173

The imitation jewels made of glass in ancient Egypt and India were almost as valuable to their owners as real ones. Many examples have been found like the one shown here — an earring made up of tiny glass beads on silver wire, with metal discs hanging from the lower arc.

Reflections and shadows of glass objects such as this can be very interesting, particularly if the glass is coloured. Try to capture shadows of this kind either by photography or a sketch on paper with pen or crayon; the results may suggest a textural or background treatment, or even a complete design if the shadows or reflections are sharp enough.

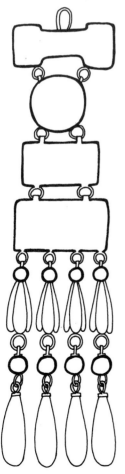

172

A simplified drawing of a gold pendant found in a tomb at Monte Alban in South America suggests an interesting way to present a series of small, related panels. The original, elaborate pendant is of Mixtec art of the eighth to eleventh centuries AD; the panels were of a related size and design, which is one reason why it looks so complete and well-balanced.

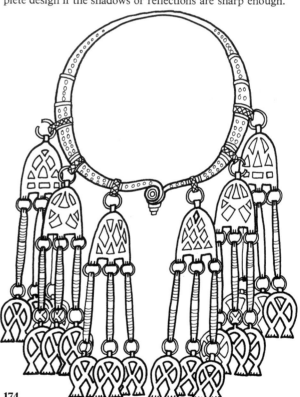

174

For those who enjoy macramé, a neck ring like the one shown here may provide the starting point for a new project. this one, with conical ends and pendants attached, was made in western Lithuania around AD 300. It could be used equally well as a design for surface stitchery, using covered rings in the appropriate places; or even taken to pieces and each piece used separately; or with the number of pendants increased and positioned to radiate from the neck ring to form a circular design.

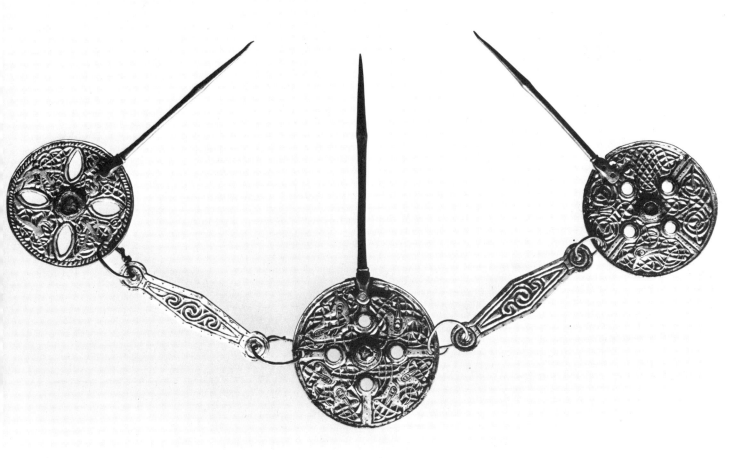

175
Anglo-Saxon triple pin brooch (see **170**) from Witham near Lincoln (British Museum).

176
These beads, made and used by people today, are of exactly the same materials used thousands of years ago. They come from many countries, and include pieces of glass, turquoise, amber, jade, ivory, shell, stone, bone, teeth, wood and seeds. Many of these shapes can be made at home in quick-drying clay, then painted, varnished and used in embroidery. Others may suggest stitchery patterns and ways of ornamenting small surfaces.

Remember to look out for little things like these in museums, and make a note of their shapes, colours and materials, and the way they are strung together.

Buildings and mosaics

Brick and stonework patterns often suggest interesting arrangements for patchwork; the ones here can be used for that purpose as well as for some counted thread methods of embroidery.

Rooftops sometimes have patterned tiles which can be very decorative, especially those of different colours laid in zig-zags to form a pattern looking like Florentine stitch. Some old roofs have curved tiles set in a circular formation, and those of some ancient temples have domes which are a great favourite among embroiderers, as are the towers and minarets of Islamic architecture.

Old Indian temples are so crowded with carved figures and designs that the impression is one of texture rather than one particular element. Often these crowded designs form vertical and horizontal rows resembling beading, plaiting and smocking.

Windows and pavements show carefully laid out pieces of glass and stone. Look carefully at their arrangements and make sketches for future reference, or photograph them. They may be just what you need for a patchwork project.

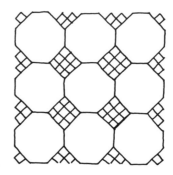

177
This design is from a brick pavement of the Roman period now in Reading Museum, England. It could be rendered either in blackwork or in patchwork. Imagine this design used on a bedspread: the octagons of a mid-brown, thick, silky fabric and the small squares in a riot of brilliant jewel colours.

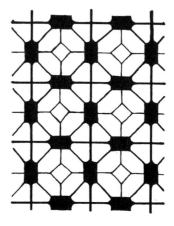

178
Windows in ancient buildings are well known to embroiderers as sources of ideas for blackwork stitches. This design is from a window in the nave of the Palatine Chapel at Palermo in Sicily, built in the twelfth century.

179
The octagonal mosaic design dates from about the fourth century AD and was made for the Church of St. Costanza in Rome.
  It may suggest a patchwork cushion of brilliant colours.

180
This single motif from a Byzantine mosaic in the Galla Placidia, Ravenna, has a snowflake quality and would indeed be very effective embroidered in white, grey and black on a dark grey background, or in one other main colour with white and black.
  The actual colours of the mosaic are yellow, white, black, blue, green and grey on a purple background; although this sounds rather too much for one small motif, the predominance of yellow in fact balanced the other colours very well.

181
Tiny square *tesserae* inspired this piece of stitchery which is made up of little blocks of colour and pattern in the style of many mosaic borders. The embroiderer, Audrey Ormrod, chose a loosely woven cream cotton material which looked as though threads had been withdrawn from it; she then threaded the fabric with wools of several thicknesses in deep yellow, chestnut brown and black. Some stranded embroidery cotton and Anchor soft cotton were used, as well as a narrow braid which can be seen just below the centre of the photograph.

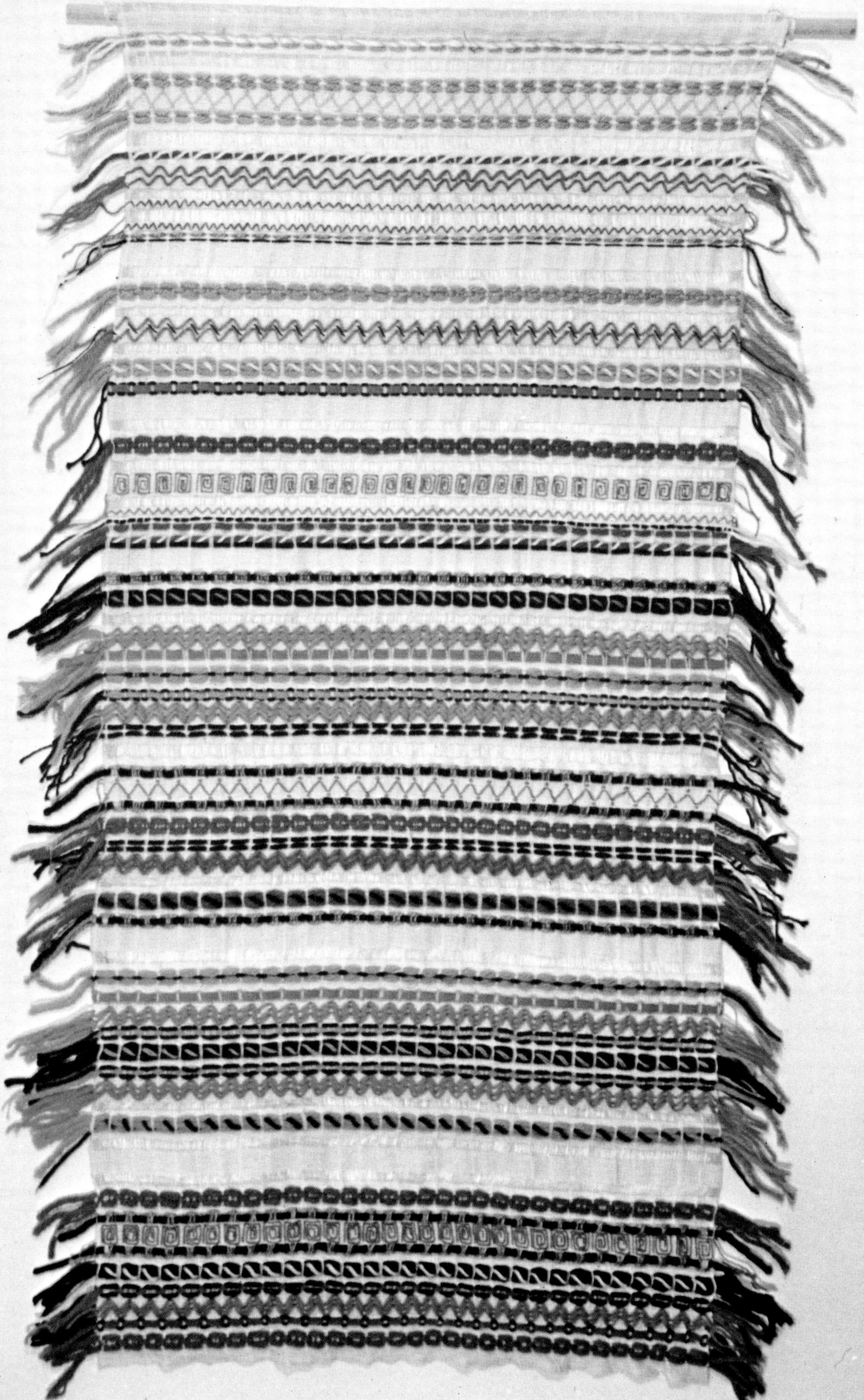

Mosaics are made by placing cubes of coloured stone, marble, pottery or glass on to a bed of damp plaster to form a pattern. Of the various types of ancient mosaic work, Roman, Byzantine and Aztec are probably the most familiar. We remember the Romans mainly for their ceramic pavements, many of which still exist, for instance in England at Cirencester, London, Lincoln and Leicester, and in Italy at the ruins of Pompeii.

Byzantine artists demonstrated their skill in the art of mosaic work on the walls of churches throughout the Byzantine Empire, and on pavements too. Their processions of emperors and courtiers are masterpieces of intricate detail and brilliant colour. The material used for the finest wall panels was glass, but porphyry, serpentine and white

182
The Romans excelled in the art of mosaic making. This one, said to have come from Populonia near Rome, dates from the second century AD, and is made of coloured marbles. (Reproduced by kind permission of the Victoria and Albert Museum, London.) The very nature of the material used (square *tesserae*) lends an unmistakably strong design appearance to every creature and even to the beautifully mottled background. Notice particularly the lobster, the fish just to the left of its left antenna, and the eel; these show great delicacy and clever arrangement of light and shade to suggest both pattern and shape.

marble were also used for the decoration of other objects in mosaic. Gold leaf was sometimes fused between two pieces of glass to give a rich glow.

Mosaics take a three-dimensional form in Aztec art, covering knife handles, skulls and masks. On a much smaller scale than either the Roman or Byzantine mosaics, they are nevertheless brilliant, using turquoise and jade, red and white shell, pyrites and jet. The pieces are also more irregular in size and shape, creating a very interesting effect.

Textiles

The first looms were probably tied to trees at one end, and at the other to logs on the ground. They may also, in some parts of the world, have consisted of horizontally stretched warps lying very close to the ground between two logs. Both vertical and horizontal looms of the most primitive kind are still used in many countries today, to produce some of the finest and most technically excellent cloth to be seen anywhere in the world. Both plain and complex weaves are used, with patterns of many colours and designs. Samples of these can be seen in museums of ethnography, where they are an inspiration to designers and craftsmen.

Also used, both by the very earliest *and* present-day weaver, is the back-strap loom; this loom is anchored at one end to the branch of a tree or some other stable object (I use the knob at the bottom of the staircase), while the other warp ends are fastened to a stick which is in turn fastened across the front of the weaver's waist by a strap. The weaver can then adjust the tension of the warps as he or she leans forward or backward against the strap. Weaving starts at the end nearest the weaver, who rolls up the woven area, as it is produced, around the stick at the waist, tying another stick on top of this to prevent it unrolling. For thousands of years the weavers of Peru have used this type of loom to produce fabric which has never been surpassed in quality by any other nation.

The study of Oriental carpets and rugs is fascinating and rewarding, for it not only enables you to recognize examples in museums, houses and antique shops, but gives you a completely new insight into the way of life of the people who make them. The geography of the countries of origin, the lifestyles of the nomadic or semi-nomadic weavers, the symbolic significance of the motifs used by them — all these aspects of the subject are of interest to designers who like to know a little about the ideas they are interpreting.

183

Log cabin patchwork is constructed in a series of 'logs' laid from a central square outwards, with each end overlapping the previous one in the manner of a spiral. Tones are traditionally arranged so that light and dark lie on diagonally opposite sides to represent the glow of the fire lighting one half of the room, casting the other half into shadow.

On this bedspread the squares have been arranged to form larger squares of light and dark. The design is reminiscent of brick and stonework patterns on Persian buildings, and on decorated ceilings, roofs and tiled pavements. (Reproduced by kind permission of the Pitt-Rivers Museum, Oxford.)

The traditional arrangement of light and dark need not, of course, be retained in every piece of work. Some other exciting variations can be found — perhaps padding each strip as it is laid down, or having a light colour for the central square, shading to a very dark one on the outside edge, or vice versa.

Canvas embroidery or Pulled Thread

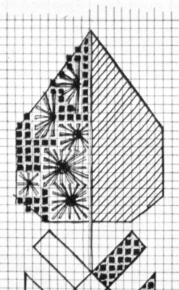

Eyelets

Drawn-
buttonhole filling
or
Diagonal cross
filling

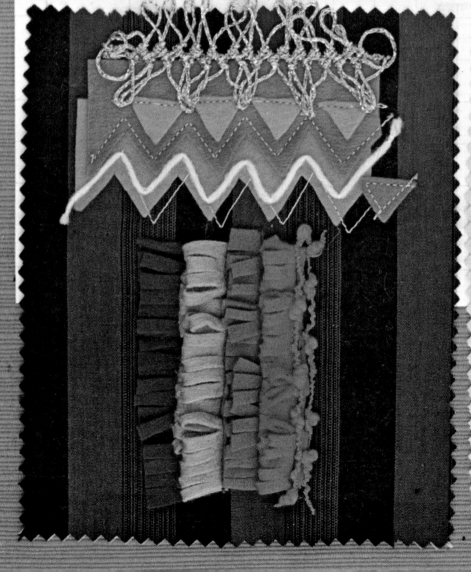

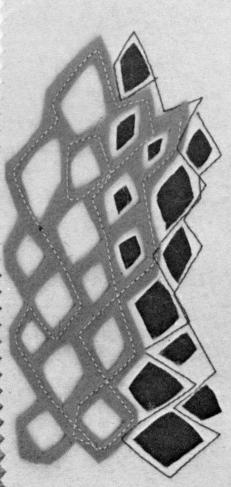

The Maoris of New Zealand are responsible for the invention of a finger-weaving technique called Taniko (or Taaniko). In New Zealand its original use was for capes and cloaks with gaily coloured borders in beautiful geometric patterns. Modern uses for Taniko weaving include bodices, belts and headbands which form part of the traditional Maori costume.

The colours of the design shown here are red, white and a very little yellow on a dark blue background. The natural cream of the unbleached flax is a predominant colour in many of these designs.

184

Notebook page and samples based on **189**. Very often one can find small exciting details on woven textiles which lend themselves in some way to other textile techniques. These may be interpreted on small samples and kept together in a notebook for reference.

The carpet from Fars is packed with little trees, plants and flowers, animals, birds and charming little figures. The geometrical nature of these motifs makes them easy to adapt to a counted-thread technique such as pulled-thread or canvas embroidery. Zig-zag and striped patterns may be expressed in more unusual ways too, making use of the sewing-machine to sew down strips of rolled and cut felt, and for holding down a network of felt in three tones.

186

Here is a design which I have adapted from a motif in the oldest known carpet in the world—the Pazyryk carpet. It was discovered in a Scythian burial site at Pazyryk in Central Mongolia, and it dates from about 500 BC. It had apparently been used as a saddle cloth; it is finely knotted, and probably of Babylonian or Persian origin.

This part of the design comes from the wide border on the outer edge which consists of horses and riders. It was adapted with canvas embroidery in mind, but would work equally well in some other counted thread method.

You will probably already know that originally carpets fulfilled a different role from that of floor covering. Instead, they covered walls to keep draughty castle rooms warm, as well as covering tables and beds. The knotted and looped pile rugs and carpets of the nomadic tribes of Persia and Central Asia, too, are not only used on floors but also for decorating the walls of tents; as cushions, when stuffed; as tent bags to hold belongings, as we would use chests of drawers; as covers for carts and wagons, as camel-, horse- and donkey-bags for carrying luggage, including children; and as saddle cloths. Prayer rugs are used by Moslems as protection from the bare ground when saying prayers out-of-doors.

The origin of pile fabrics is very ancient, and although it is difficult to say whether the very earliest recorded carpets were loop pile or knotted pile, we do know that the weaving techniques used to produce carpet knotting go as far back as prehistoric times. They are made on both horizontal and vertical looms, and are woven mostly by women and children, who find it easier to manipulate the threads with their small, nimble fingers. Various methods are used in different countries to produce rough-faced and smooth-faced pile, and the materials vary between wool and cotton (which are sometimes used together), camel wool, goat hair and silk.

The dyes used to produce the rich colours associated with Oriental carpets came originally from vegetable sources. Indeed this is still the origin of many of the dyes used today by handworkers, nomads and semi-nomads, who produce them from such exotic sounding sources as the stamens of the saffron flower, vine leaves, pomegranates, madder, gall nut, seashells and betel shells. Because of the nomadic existence of many of these carpet makers, they often produce only small amounts of any one particular dye for immediate use, and make another lot when it is required on the next occasion. This means that there is sometimes quite a noticeable colour variation in the same carpet which, to those who understand why, adds to its attraction. The machine-made ones do not have these irregularities, nor do you find any distortion or imperfection in the design as you often do on those made by hand. I find these little 'mistakes' quite charming; I would go so far as to suggest that one or two irregularities of this nature would not come amiss on similar pieces of work made by embroiderers. Is this taking borrowed ideas too far? I think not as long as the 'deliberate mistakes' are bold enough not to look like real errors in workmanship.

187
Patterns from a border design which suggest padded or quilted shapes, or brightly coloured appliqué with surface stitchery. The design comes from a first-century woven woollen rug from Central Asia.

188
An Anatolian carpet design showing the battle of the dragon and the phoenix; this has become so stylized that it is now almost abstract. It is an example of a motif being distorted to make it fit into a shape. It is, however, very decorative and well-balanced, and makes a very pleasing arrangement which may give embroiderers ideas for similar exercises.

189
A carpet from Fars in Persia, made in the nineteenth or twentieth century, showing an abundance of little figures, trees, plants and animals. (Victoria and Albert Museum.)

110

190

This canvas-work panel measures 13.7 x 20 in. (35 x 51 cm.), and is worked in colours ranging from white through all shades of pink, mauve, purple and crimson; silver thread and kid were also used. The intention was to create a brilliant glow of bright colours on and immediately around the figure, contrasting with a very dark crimson and purple background.

Most of the stitches are conventional canvas-work stitches, except those outlining the curves, which are of chain stitch. Tufting is used on the head-dress, the wrists, the overskirt and the shoes; the belt and part of the helmet are of padded silver kid, giving a smooth, shining effect.

191

This detail of the canvas-work panel shows the overskirt, which is made of tiny plaits of many different threads inserted from the back of the canvas and finished off at the bottom in the same way. The line of tufting covers the bottom of the plaits. The large square eyelets which hang down the front are worked so that the last stitches cover the first ones and cast an interesting shadow effect on each one.

192
Tie-dye silk textile of the twentieth century from India.
(Victoria and Albert Museum).

Faces and figures

Artists as far back in time as the Stone Age have
been preoccupied with portraying man as the
hunter, and woman as a general fertility figure,
rather than any one person in particular. Since then,
many styles have evolved and changed from impres-
sionism to realism to abstraction and back again,
depending on the material, the purpose and the
tradition. The human figure can be seen portrayed
in every conceivable medium, including wood and
stone, metal and clay (both moulded and painted),
all kinds of textiles, basketwork, mosaics, sand- and
wall-paintings. All these media impose restrictions
on the artist which affect the style of his work to a
lesser or greater degree. The embroiderer must also
recognize that there are limitations to embroidery,
too, since by its very nature it interprets ideas best as
design and not in the style of naturalistic pictures.
Therefore the human figure too, must be treated as
design, and we must find a way of incorporating
certain necessary degrees of movement, emotion
and other human qualities while still retaining that
element of un-realism.

193
The tapestries of the Coptic weavers show some very
beautiful, soulful faces like the one here of St Theodore.
It is very similar in style to portraits of the Byzantine era
with very large and clearly defined features from which a
design can readily be adapted. In my drawing, I have
created harder edges to the areas of shadow than were
actually there.

114

Contradictory as it may seem, this can best be achieved by studying and making many sketches of the human body from life. There is no better way to understand the proportions, the formation of angles and curves, the balance, and the possibilities of position and movement of which the body is capable. In this subject above all others, the embroiderer who has seen and noted the moving parts will excel, even though she may use sources for her designs which come from other times and other countries.

When looking at a particular source of inspiration for a human figure design, try to pick out the general shapes as geometrical forms, and the flow of lines which follow through them. Break the composition down into geometrical sections and adjust the balance and arrangement of limbs to convey the impression you require—not necessarily the same one as the source you are using. Remember that it is only an idea of shape, treatment or feeling which you are borrowing, not an exact replica.

Details of facial features, hands, feet, even arms may be omitted if the designer wishes to concentrate the attention on another part of the body; the human form need not retain its symmetry. Only those parts which are necessary to the design need be included, along with other extra lines and shapes which will help to convey and exaggerate any of the human qualities mentioned previously, or which will help the balance of the design.

194
The Neo-Assyrian head of Sargon II is from an alabaster relief from Khorsabad (721–705 BC). Here the accent is on the decorative treatment of the hair and beard, with a richly jewelled headband for contrast both in pattern and direction. There is no suggestion of shadow or depth, but what an exciting opportunity for an embroiderer to use her skill on this kind of design.

195
The famous Byzantine mosaics offer a wide variety of figures for study, many of them beautifully colourful and decorative, or covered with patterns, like this figure from the west wall of the Cathedral at Torcello, Italy, which dates from the twelfth century. It could inspire embroiderers with ideas for a richly patterned figure using a combination of methods—perhaps hardanger embroidery or needleweaving with appliqué or quilting. An interesting textural effect on parts of the robe could be achieved by some pleating and smocking.

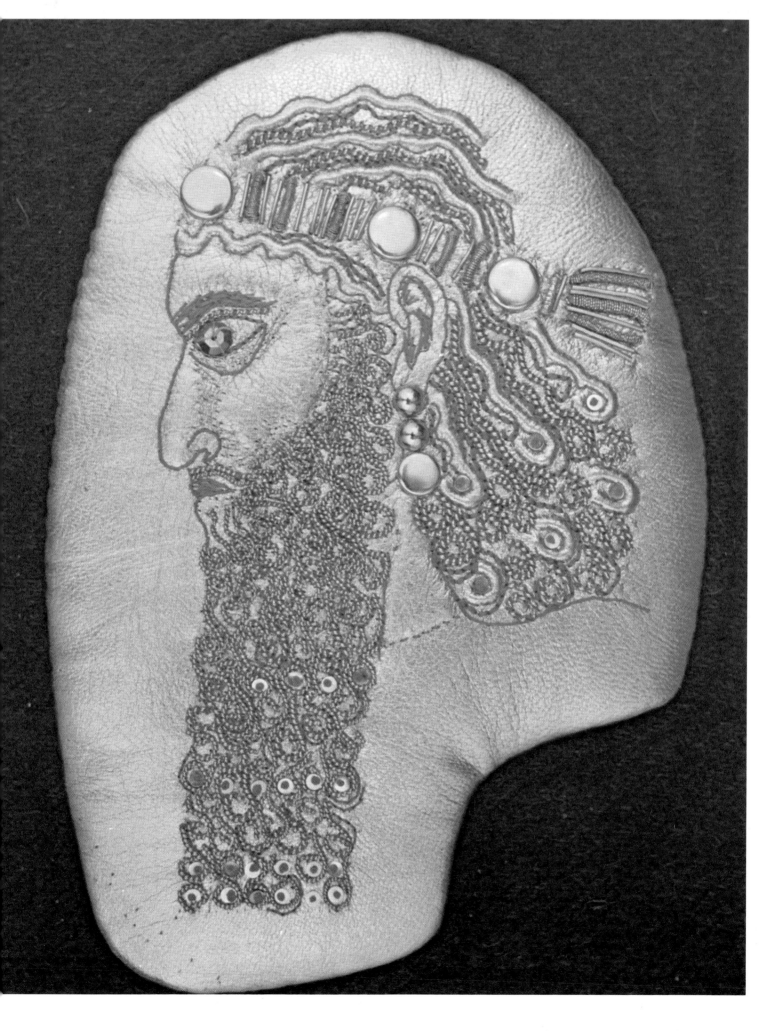

196

The skilful use of gold shows how the design of the head of Sargon II has been brought to life by Val Harding. Worked on gold kid, the head measures 6 in. (15.2 cm.) from the crown to the bottom edge of the beard. The hair is suggested by corded quilting and gold purl couched down with orange silk, and on the beard tiny sequins have been used in rows fastened down with french knots. The face has been slightly padded, and the headband and earrings are small gold studs and smooth and rough purl.

197

Canvas embroidery based on **199**. The Standard of Ur is richly covered with little figures, but the one from the top left hand corner appealed to me particularly because of his decorative dress. He adapted easily to canvas embroidery, as he shows both profile and full face in the manner of ancient Egyptian wall paintings, and so presents a square image. The mosaic pieces in the background also adapt well to various canvas stitches. The body is worked in bricking stitch, a form of Gobelin stitch, and all the black areas are tent stitch to accentuate the textured panels.

The complete panel measures 9 x 6½ in. (19 x 16.5 cm.). This mosaic scene made of shell and lapis lazuli set in bitumen comes from a small chest, known as 'The Standard of Ur' from Mesopotamia, *c*2780 BC.

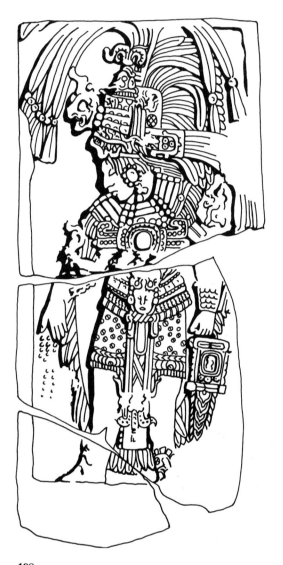

198
The Mayas of Central America left behind them huge stones, or stelae, on which they had carved the mose complicated and intricate designs. Alongside the hieroglyphics are gods with feathered head-dresses, and scrolls in such abundance that it is difficult to sort out the beginnings and ends of figures. I used this drawing as a source of inspiration for a panel worked in canvas embroidery.

The treatment of faces in embroidery must, of course, be strictly in keeping with the treatment of the rest of the figure, unless the design is of a head or face by itself when the method of embroidery will, to a large extent, dictate the shape of the features and the degree of detail possible. Embroiderers and designers will appreciate that it is quite inconsistent to treat the figure in a flat, decorative manner and then shade the face carefully in long and short stitch to suggest moulded contours.

Primitive and ancient sources are particularly useful for ideas of heads and faces as they are often treated in a two-dimensional way and are therefore reasonably simple to transpose into an embroidery technique. Apart from this aspect, many examples also have a decorative quality, a freedom from the restrictions of realism, and an uninhibited child-like gaiety. A study of faces, heads and head-dresses can provide us with an almost unlimited supply of ideas—those of the Ancient Egyptians, for example, and the wildly exciting head-dresses (and costumes too) of contemporary primitive societies.

Creatures and plants

Embroiderers who need inspiration for a design of an animal can do no better than to study works of primitive and ancient origin, for animals have always been a favourite subject among artists from the very earliest times. The beautiful creatures drawn on the cave walls of Altamira and Lascaux prove that skill in drawing has not evolved in the same way as many other skills; the beauty of the work has depended solely on the ability of the artist, and apparently there was such ability *then* as there is *now*.

The study of live animals may seem irrelevant if you need a design of a mythical creature, but it helps to show where legs and head are placed in relation to the rest of the body even though, in design, the limbs may be exaggerated. It also helps the designer to see what can and cannot be done with the contortions (for design purposes) of an animal's body, with the correct proportions of such details as wings, spines, claws, fangs and scales coming from the 'right' places.

199
Standard of Ur. (British Museum).

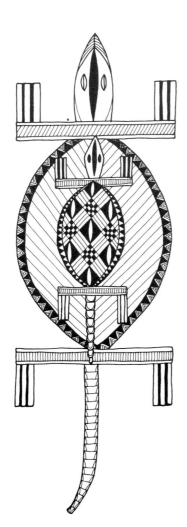

200
This dragon is taken from a drawing of a rubbing from one side of a stone sarcophagus found at Lu Shan in China, dated AD 212. He is a splendid, sinewy creature; no wonder that the dragon of the Han dynasty was adopted as the national and imperial symbol.

Notice that the dragon is not covered all over with pattern; the line of the body, neck and tail are enough indication of his beauty. To do too much to a good design tends to 'gild the lily'.

201
The shape of this lizard has been simplified to such a degree that it becomes a geometric form with an exact replica of itself on its back. The two lizards make a design perfect for embroidery. They come from a carved door of a house in the Nupe town of Lapai in northern Nigeria.

119

Birds and fish, too, are a favourite source of design to artists and craftsmen, both past and present, for their compact shapes and ornamental markings make them ideal models for almost any medium. Consequently they are found in very many styles of art, offering an almost unlimited range of treatments.

For embroiderers, the few shown here may suggest ideas from which to construct a design. Do not let anyone put you off with, 'Oh, but *everyone* does fish and birds!' If *you* have not, and would like to, then go ahead and prove that no one has yet produced one as beautiful and original as yours.

More fish and bird ideas can be found in other sections of this book, but for still more ideas look at Egyptian wall paintings, ancient jewelry, finials, handles and lids, manuscripts and stone carvings, Greek vases, textiles and pottery of ancient and primitive origin, and coins and mosaics.

Studying plants from ancient and primitive sources gives us a chance to see the various stages of their evolution from the natural and three-dimensional to the flat, stylized and sometimes abstract form. Plant forms do not abound in contemporary primitive art except in certain areas such as the islands of, Sumatra and Borneo, where the plant motifs are delightfully abstracted to conform to the traditional textile art. Most other primitive societies seem to be far more concerned with animal, human and geometric figures than with plant life, unlike the ancients in whose work it often appeared as part of the scene set for the purposes of recounting an historical occasion.

The Ancient Egyptians included lush plant life in their wall paintings, reliefs, and enamels, and the Assyrians, too, showed a similar love of scene-setting in their use of trees, reeds, grasses and other foliage.

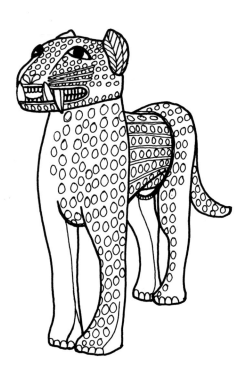

203
A bird design can become so stylized that it is almost abstract, like this little creature from the top of a round Chinese bronze vessel of the Early Chou period, around 1122 BC. It would adapt very well to a design for canvas or pulled thread work because of its angularity, or could be used equally successfully as a motif for goldwork.

204
Two trees based on **205**. This small experiment shows two completely different interpretations of the trees seen on the Assyrian relief.

The one on the left is of brown felt appliquéd on to a background of furnishing fabric; an angular design accentuated by cream textured wool couched along some edges. The small circles are filled with tiny french knots and the centre trunk is marked by a chain stitch.

The tree on the right exaggerates the original curves by the use of a bumpy cream silk thread which creates more impact by texture than by colour. Wools and silks of various thicknesses are used in a few stitches: knotted cable stitch, french knots and chain stitch for the trunk.

Each tree measures 7½ in. (19cm.) high. They were embroidered by the author.

202
This leopard is one of a well-known pair of African ivory leopards which stand in the Museum of Mankind, London. Like the lion, other members of the cat family have always been well represented in ancient and primitive art. This one has brass studs for spots, neatly placed in rows.

Do sketch animals whenever and wherever you see them. A page of a diary or a paper bag will do in the absence of your sketch book—much better than trying to remember an interesting detail several weeks later and not being able to. Even a rough sketch will help to remind you, and this may make a big difference to your basic design.

205
Assyrian relief from the palace of Sennacherib at Nineveh,
*c*650 BC (British Museum).

206

Reminiscent of the designs on the Chilkat blankets of the Tlingit group of American Indians, this killer whale design belongs to a related group, the Haida, who also live on the Northwest Pacific coast. Its clearly-marked curves create a smooth and sleek line which is typical of the killer whale.

207

You can sometimes create an interesting idea for a background by superimposing one design on top of another. In this case, the cock was traced and placed over a drawing of gauze weave, which provided an impression of grasses arranged in a slightly formal manner; this seems to be in keeping both with the style of the bird and the subject matter. The motif originated from a Sassanian silk textile of the sixth to seventh centuries AD, which may have been woven in Persia. Textiles of the Byzantine era abound with decorative birds and animals.

208

Old illuminated manuscripts are rich sources of ideas for weird and fantastic animals, birds and fish. This little roundel is from a painted manuscript of the eighth century AD. Similar round designs contain human and animal figures which could be used on embroidered greetings cards, or, in the case of these fish, on church embroidery.

Plants of all kinds have been a favourite source of inspiration to embroiderers and textile workers throughout the ages, and though it is indeed important that the live plant should be studied and sketched with great care the examples created by ancient peoples and primitive societies, such as those of the nomadic Persian carpet-makers, may give us some ideas for decorative treatments and help us to develop our own designs for embroidery.

Plants can also be found on the pottery of the ancient Cretans, and on jewelry and wall paintings, though on the latter it looked very stiff and unhappy as though included as an afterthought.

In later eras foliage was used in abundance on church stone carvings and capitals; the more ancient and formal examples of this, however, can be seen on the Corinthian capitals of Classical Greece and the lotus flower capitals of Ancient Egypt.

209

This Egyptian glass fish, made around 1400 BC, was found at el-Amarna, the city founded by Akhenaten. Like the other small vases made of this kind of glass, it looks remarkably like Florentine stitch, though it could equally well be worked in quilting or patchwork.

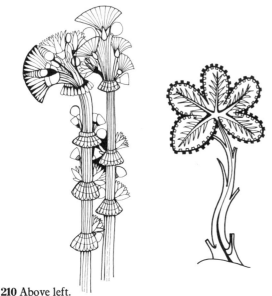

210 Above left.
One of the best-known plants of Ancient Egypt, and one which is seen repeatedly in the art of that country, is the papyrus, which was used in the making of paper as far back as the fourth millennium BC. This drawing is a detail from a painted ivory plaque in the centre of the lid of a small chest. The papyrus is a delightful plant to draw, and should be equally delightful to embroider. As an interesting experiment, turn the book upside down and see the drawing as hanging bundles of thread. All kinds of ideas are born in this way, sometimes with the most unexpected results.

211 Above right.
Many Byzantine mosaics have designs of foliage which are often quite easy to develop since they are already flat and decorative rather than naturalistic. The tree shown here is a detail from a twelfth century mosaic in the Cathedral of Monreale, a few miles south of Palermo in Sicily.

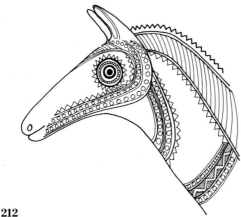

212
Toy shapes are always enhanced if the embroidery on them follows the natural lines of the body and is of a related size and shape. Very large, bold patterns on a small toy will tend to engulf it; similarly a tiny pattern on a large toy animal may be rather ineffective. Whether the toy is for a child's use or merely for decoration, will to a large extent determine the type of embroidery used on it.
This beautiful decoration on a horse's head is the Bronze Age Trundholm Horse in Demark. Though the incised lines are now only faintly visible, the pattern can still be seen looking like fine embroidery, following the curve of the horse's head and neck with a decorative collar for extra effect.

Toys

It is sometimes difficult to decide who derives the most pleasure from a handmade toy, the one who makes it or the one who plays with it. If we also add to these two the pleasure of giving, we must make sure that, if the toy is for a child, it has no bits and pieces to come loose, no sharp decorations such as sequins, beads, wire or metal threads—and it must be sturdily made.

In the past, as in some countries today, toys have been made from almost every imaginable material, including dried and plaited leaves, corncobs, moss (the Russian moss dolls of the late nineteenth century), fir cones and even tiny grains of rice!

From the very earliest times, children all over the world have found pleasure in simple and even crude replicas of themselves. This is no less true of children today, in spite of the recent influx of plastic dolls. Whilst not recommending to embroiderers the use of quite such perishable materials, much use *can* be made of materials which impart uniqueness and originality to a toy, thereby making it completely personal—materials such as leather of all kinds (suede, imitation leather and chamois), feathers, fur, old nylon tights and stockings, wood, bells and other well-made decorations. Look at the photograph of 'found' objects at the beginning of this book; they may give you some ideas for decorating toys, or even suggest the kind of toy to be made.

Almost every section in this book will provide the embroiderer with ideas which can be used on toys; the illustrations of ceramics offer particularly good ideas (little felt houses complete with little felt figures); see also the sections covering birds, animals, fish and masks.

As well as the more usual type of stuffed toy or doll figure, many ideas from ancient and primitive sources would adapt well to mobiles, glove puppets and finger puppets. These can look beautiful when embroidered with appropriate and clever designs, using sequins and beads. Many techniques can be used too, if you are careful to choose the right design and purpose for the method you wish to employ. Patchwork is very effective, as are quilting, stitches which create pile, small areas of weaving, knitting, crochet and macramé, metal thread embroidery and appliqué. Here is a chance to make use of all kinds of colourful 'fun' decorations, such as shisha glass, metal studs, plastic netting, shells and imitation jewels.

Always try to look for the main idea when studying a source of inspiration, rather than wondering how you can make an exact copy of it.

124

Alter the design where you need to, but always aim to retain the characteristic features. Several ideas can be used from different sources to create a design for one toy, but I would strongly suggest that a working drawing is made before starting to cut or sew, as this will help you to ensure that your ideas are workable.

214a and b

Ideas for toy decoration can be seen on bronze statuettes from many countries. In these two from Nigeria the lines of the pattern follow the shape of the animal's back, and can either be worked in surface embroidery by hand or machine, or by using buttonholed curtain rings sewn to strips of fabric, tiny plastic washers sewn down with metal-thread, and shisha glass insets. Metal or hand-made cords can be couched down to form patterns, finished off with free-hanging objects, tassels or pom-poms. Scroll-work areas can be couched too, perhaps with metal threads to match the cord, or silk of a contrasting colour.

213

A puppet doll, or perhaps a hanging one, can be made in the style of the Navaho sand-paintings. These are representations of gods and goddesses, spirits and sacred places. The designs are formed by sprinkling coloured powders made from charcoal, pulverized minerals of different colours, corn-meal, pollen and dried flower-petals on to a bed of sand.

215

Ideas for dolls can often be found by looking at old museum-pieces, even though they may be well-worn and faded. Little costume details and accessories can be noted for use on a hand-made doll which need not necessarily represent any particular country or era.

The drawing here was made from an old Persian doll; the style of her clothes makes an interesting change from the more usual European dress. The head ornaments lend an eastern flavour and a colourful focal point.

216 Above right.

This doll with long pendant earrings is based on a very dilapidated museum-piece from Arabia. She could become either a complete doll or a glove puppet.

Bibliography

Ancient art

Aldred, Cyril *Tutankhamun's Egypt,* B.B.C. London 1972.
Belloni, Gian Guido and Dall'Asen, Liliana *Iranian Art,* Pall Mall Press, London 1969; Praeger, New York.
Bushnell, G. H. S. *Ancient Arts of the Americas,* Thames and Hudson, London 1968; Praeger, New York.
Bushnell, G. H. S. *The First Americans,* Thames and Hudson, London 1968; McGraw Hill, New York.
Enciso, Jorge *Design Motifs of Ancient Mexico,* Constable, London 1947; Dover, New York.
Gimbutas, Marija *The Balts,* Thames and Hudson, London 1963; Praeger, New York.
Hope, Thomas *Costumes of the Greeks and Romans,* Constable, London 1962; Dover, New York.
Jenkins, G. K. *Ancient Greek Coins,* Barrie and Jenkins, London 1972.
Larousse Encyclopaedia of Byzantine and Medieval Art, Hamlyn, London 1968; Putnam, New York.
Lommel, Andreas and others *The Stone Age,* 'Art of the World' Series, Methuen, London 1960.
MacCana, Proinsias *Celtic Mythology,* Hamlyn, London 1969; Tudor, New York.
Mason, J. Alden *The Ancient Civilizations of Peru,* Penguin, Harmondsworth 1969.
Quennell, Marjorie and C. B. H. *Everyday Life in Anglo-Saxon Times,* (and many others in the 'Everyday Life' series) Batsford, revised edition, London 1959; Putnam, New York 1960.
Rosenthal, Renate *Jewellery in Ancient Times,* Cassell, London 1973.
Talbot Rice, D. *Art of the Byzantine Era,* Thames and Hudson, London 1970; Praeger, New York.
Willetts, William *Chinese Art, Book I,* Penguin, Harmondsworth 1958.

Primitive art

Adam, L. D. *Primitive Art,* Penguin, Harmondsworth 1940; Baines & Noble, New York 1963.
Ambesi, A. C. *Oceanic Art,* Hamlyn, London 1966; Tudor, New York.
Barrow, T. *Decorative Arts of the New Zealand Maori,* A. H. and A. W. Reed, Wellington, Sydney and London 1964.
Boas, Franz *Primitive Art,* Dover, New York 1955; Constable, London.
Haberland, W. *North America,* 'Art of the World' Series, Methuen, London 1968.
Larousse Encyclopaedia of Primitive and Prehistoric Art, Hamlyn, London 1968.
Leuzinger, E. *The Art of Black Africa,* Studio Vista, London 1972; N.Y.G.S., New York.
Lommel, Andreas *Prehistoric and Primitive Man,* Hamlyn, London 1966.
Sides, Dorothy S. *Decorative Arts of the South Western Indians,* Dover, New York 1962; Constable, London.
Willett, Frank *African Art,* Thames and Hudson, London 1971; Praeger, New York.

General

Con, J. M. *Carpets from the Orient,* Merlin Press, London 1966; Universe, New York.
Hill, Derek and Oleg Grabar *Islamic Architecture and its Decoration,* Faber, London 1965; University of Chicago Press, Chicago.
Koch, Rudolf *The Book of Signs,* Dover, New York 1955.
Lommel, Andreas, *Masks,* Elek, London 1972.
Meyer, Franz. S. *Handbook of Ornament,* Dover, New York 1957.
Rare Carpets, Orbis, London 1972; Crown, New York.
Reed, Stanley *Oriental Carpets and Rugs,* Octopus, London 1972; Putnam, New York.
Speltz, Alexander *The Styles of Ornament,* Dover, New York 1959; Constable, London.

Embroidery

Clucas, Joy *Your Machine for Embroidery,* Bell, London 1973.
Dawson, Barbara *Metal Thread Embroidery,* Batsford, London 1968; Taplinger, New York.
de Dillmont, Thérèse *The Complete Encyclopedia of Needlework,* D.M.C. London 1972; Running Press, USA.
Dyer, A. and Duthoit, V. *Canvas Work from the Start,* Bell, London 1972.
Edson, Nicki Mitz and Stimmel, Arlene *Creative Crochet,* Pitman, London 1973.
Feldman, Dol Pitt *The Crocheter's Art/New Dimensions in Free Form Crochet,* Nelson, London and New York 1975.
Green, Sylvia *Canvas Embroidery for Beginners,* Studio Vista, London 1970; Watson-Guptill, New York.
Liley, Alison *Embroidery—A Fresh Approach,* Mills and Boon, London 1964.
Liley, Alison *The Craft of Embroidery,* Mills and Boon, London 1961.
Mon Tricot Knitting Dictionary: 1030 Stitches and Patterns, Condé Nast Publications, London and New York.
Short, Jacqueline *Macramé, the Craft of Knotting,* Blandford Press, London 1973.
Snook, Barbara *Embroidery Stitches,* Batsford, London 1963.
Thomas, Mary *Mary Thomas's Embroidery Book,* Hodder and Stoughton, London 1936.
Wilson, Jean *Weaving is for Anyone,* Studio Vista, London; Van Nostrand Reinhold, New York 1967.
Wilson, Jean *Weaving is Creative,* Van Nostrand Reinhold, New York 1972.
Znamierowski, Nell *Rugmaking,* Pan, London 1972.

Suppliers

Great Britain

Send a stamped, addressed envelope for price lists and samples.

Ordinary needlework supplies
All thread, wools, silks, cotton and metal (gold, silver, etc.). Linens and sewing accessories.
  Mace and Nairn, 89 Crane Street, Salisbury, Wiltshire.

Rug-making supplies
Rug wool and thrums, canvas and tools.
  Jackson's Rug-Craft Centre, Croft Mill, Hebden Bridge, Yorkshire.

Rug wool and thrums, knitting wool, canvas and tools.
  T. L. Winwood (Kidderminster) Carpets, P.O. Box 27, Lisle Avenue, Kidderminster, Worcestershire.

Fleece, natural materials, etc.
Spun and unspun flax, jute, ramie, hemp, many types of cord and twine for tapestry and rug-weaving and macramé.
  Mersey Yarns (Mrs. Margaret Seagroatt), 2 Staplands Road, Liverpool, L14 3LL.

Handspun wools for weavers, and fleece of various shades.
  Craftsman's Mark Ltd., Trefnant, Denbigh, N. Wales, LL16 5UD.

Unusual textured wools and yarns for embroidery
Handweaving yarns, unspun fibres both natural and synthetic. Also good value ½lb. packs of yarns for embroiderers. Wide range of colours, materials and textures.
  Yarns (R. G. C. Edwards), 21 Portland Street, Taunton, Somerset, YA1 1UY.

Wide range of textured yarns and wools by the skein of approx. 12 yds.
  Joanne Grahame, Cuyahoga Studio, 10 Wheatlands Farm Road, Kilbarchan, Renfrewshire, 10PA 2LL.

Other Materials
As well as handicraft and embroidery materials, fabrics, yarns, and accessories: beads, sequin waste, acetate squares, wood chips and discs, feathers and many other articles.
  Cotswold Craft Centre, Mrs. R. Tyley, 5 Whitehall, Stroud, Gloucestershire GL5 1HA.

Large range of felt and hessian (burlap).
  The Felt and Hessian Shop, 34 Greville Street, London, EC1.

Beads, sequins, sequin waste.
  Ells and Farrier, 5 Princes Street, Hanover Square, London W1.

Leather pieces and whole skins.
  The Light Leather Co. Ltd., 18 Newman Street, London W1.

USA

Crewel and tapestry wool.
  Appleton Brothers of London, West Main Road, Little Compton, Rhode Island 02837.

Canvas, wools and accessories.
  Bucky King Embroideries Limited, 121 South Drive, Pittsburgh, Pennsylvania 15238.

General supplies.
  Needlecraft Shop, 13561 Ventura Blvd., Sherman Oaks, California 91403.

Embroidery supplies, silks and metal threads.
  Boutique Margot, 26 W 54 Street, New York, NY 10019.

Yarns.
  Yarn Bazaar, Yarncrafts Ltd., 3146 M Street, North West Washington DC.

Burlap and felt.
  Bon Bazaar Ltd.
  149 Waverly Place, New York, NY 10014.

Beads.
  Hollander Bead & Novelty Corporation, 25 West 37 Street, New York 18, NY.

Index

Numbers in italics refer to illustrations.

Africa 69, 70; *1, 48, 102-109, 143, 144, 201, 202, 214a & b*
American Indians 28, 71, 72, 94; *5, 43, 110-115, 118, 206, 213*
Ancient Egypt 27, 28, 50, 82, 83, 99, 118, 120; *54, 71-73, 209, 210*
Anderson, Georgina, embroidery by, 138
Andrews, Christine, embroidery by, 139
Anglo Saxons 59, 63; *38, 84, 88-94, 154, 158, 159, 170, 175*
animals 118; *5, 15a, 35, 36, 54, 67, 186, 188, 200-203, 206-209, 212, 214a & b*
Assyria 27-28, 99, 120; *154, 194, 196, 204, 205*
Australia 66; *15a, 26c, 95-98*
basketry 66, 72; *115*
birds 120:*22c, 156, 157, 166, 184, 203, 207*
Bronze Age 54, 55; *81, 82a & b, 83a & b, 86, 212*
buildings 104; *165, 177, 178, 183*
Byzantine 83, 106; *180, 193, 195, 211*
calligraphy 78; *123-129*
carpets and rugs see textiles
carving 18, 24, 58, 67, 69, 123; *26c, 51, 85, 95, 99, 100, 194, 198, 205*
cave paintings 47, 50; *67-69*
Celts 26, 55, 58, 83; *87a & b, 135, 136*
ceramics 94, 99; *29, 43, 44, 76, 161-166*
China 83; *200, 203*
coins 26, 89; *151, 152, 156, 157*
drapery 24; *24, 70, 77, 78*
enlarging and reducing 36, 40, 44
fabrics 36, 45; *5, 46, 56, 59, 91, 93, 162*
faces and figures 114-115, 118; *44, 68, 73-75, 87a & b, 92, 94, 98, 101-104, 106, 119, 161-163, 189-191, 193-198*
fibres 7, 10, 11, 27; *102-104*
fish 120; *15, 43, 182, 206, 208, 209*
found objects 12-13, 70, 124; *2-6, 18, 26a, 176*
glass 99; *167-169, 171, 173*
Greece 22, 32, 51, 53; *24, 74, 76-78, 165, 166; see also coins*
ground marks *see Iron Age*
Harding, Valerie, embroidery by, 196
Iron Age 54, 55, 87, 89; *88, 89, 145-148*
jewelry 99; *22c, 40, 170, 172-176; see also Anglo Saxons, see also Ancient Egypt*
keys 91; *153, 155, 158, 159*
masks 8, 108, 109; *29, 70, 102-105*
Messent, Jan, embroidery by, *1, 69, 83a, 84, 92, 102-104, 130, 131, 158, 163, 164, 170, 190, 191, 197, 204*
metal threads and lurex 10, 27; *92, 138, 170, 190, 191, 196*
mosaics 104, 106, 107; *44, 179-182, 195, 199, 211*
Oceania 24, 69, 120; *99-101, 185*
Ormrod, Audrey, embroidery by, *181*
Parry, Jean, embroidery by, *157*
Persia 110; *44, 128, 184, 189, 207, 215*
plants 120-124; *72, 85, 204, 210, 211*
Povey, Yvonne, embroidery by, *146, 169*
Rome 51, 106; *75, 153, 177, 179, 181, 182*
seals and stamps 89; *149, 150, 160*
Sly, Cheryl, embroidery by, *96*
South America 15, 74, 75; *51, 116-122, 126, 130, 131, 150, 160, 161-164, 168, 169, 172, 190, 191, 198*
Sparks, Cynthia, embroidery by, *140, 141, 143, 144*
Stone Age 30, 54, 55, 83; *79, 80, 127*
string and cord 10, 11; *9, 16, 28, 55, 139, 142, 143*
surface stitches 24-25; *157, 163, 164, 169, 204*
symbols 78, 82-83; *52, 127, 132-134*
tassels, pom-poms and fringes 28; *1, 31, 32, 63, 104, 130, 163, 164, 191*
techniques 7, 8, 10, 14-28, 44
textiles 22, 71, 74, 75, 107, 110; *110-114, 130, 131, 184-189, 192, 193, 207*
threads 7, 10, 11, 44-45; *91, 93*
three dimensional embroidery 7, 28, 70; *30a & b, 96, 102-104, 162-164*
tie-dye and batik 36; *192*
toys 124-125; *82a & b, 212-216*
transferring the design 44
Vikings 22, 26, 58, 83; *50, 85, 155*
White Horse of Uffington *138-141, 145, 146*

Numbers in italics refer to illustrations.